The Church Gives Thanks and Remembers

THE CHURCH GIVES THANKS AND REMEMBERS

Essays on the Liturgical Year
Editor: Lawrence J. Johnson

Mark Searle
Tad Guzie
Patrick Regan, O.S.B.
Kathleen Hughes, R.S.C.J.

THE LITURGICAL PRESS
Collegeville, Minnesota

THE LITURGICAL PRESS
Collegeville, Minnesota 56321

Library of Congress Cataloging in Publication Data

Federation of Diocesan Liturgical Commissions. National
   Meeting (1983 : New Orleans, La.)
   The Church gives thanks and remembers.

   1. Church year—Congresses.   I. Johnson, Lawrence J.,
1933–   . II. Title.
BV30.F37   1983   263'.9   84-5664
ISBN 0-8146-1355-1

Contents

Foreword

At their 1980 national meeting in Sun Valley, the members of the Federation of Diocesan Liturgical Commissions requested their board of directors to ensure that "a catechesis on the liturgical year be initiated, the first aspect being a national meeting on that topic by 1985." This first step was taken in 1983 when the theme of the New Orleans national meeting was "The Liturgical Year: The Church Gives Thanks and Praise." The intent of the gathering was to explore from several perspectives the nature and effect of the liturgical year as described by the Constitution on the Sacred Liturgy. This collection contains the four major addresses presented at that meeting.

The Christian cycle of feasts and seasons is based on the weekly celebration of Sunday, the day called "the first holyday of all" by the Constitution on the Sacred Liturgy (no. 106). And yet how are we to appropriate the meaning of this day within our contemporary experience? In "Sunday: The Heart of the Liturgical Year," Mark Searle addresses this issue. After first sketching several key images of Sunday found in Christian tradition, e.g., Sunday as sabbath, Sunday as day of resurrection, etc., Dr. Searle develops a new image of Sunday, Sunday as "time of life-after-death." Sunday, he says, differs from the three-day weekend absorbed in consumerism; it is distinct from the sabbath with its emphasis on rest. Rather, Sunday celebrates "the incursion of life-after-death into the lives and history of the human race." It is a day which mirrors the life of the world to come. For this reason Sunday is a day of assembly, a day for the opening up of self to all the dimensions and needs of life, a day for encountering the Risen Christ in the many ways he is present among us. As such, Sunday is not only the "foundation and core of the whole liturgical year" (Constitution on the Sacred Liturgy, no. 106), but is also, contends Dr. Searle, "the heart of Christian life itself." It is, in fact, a sacrament of the Christian life.

The celebration of Sunday and of the whole liturgical calendar is rooted in the past history of a community which constantly recalls the historical works of God among his people. There can be no Christian community without a shared memory. Yet memory implies more than chance recollection of the past. Festal memory is an intersection of past, present, and future. These are the dimensions explored by Tad Guzie in "Liturgical Year: What Does It Mean to Remember?" Remembering, he says, is characteristic of human festivity and celebration: it is by sharing in the past that we escape from individualism, that we are led into the future, that we are endowed with a past history that springs us into the future. The collective act of remembering underlies our liturgical passage of time. It is the theme of joyous expectation which challenges present presuppositions and pushes us onward in hope. The liturgical calendar, concludes Dr. Guzie, "is and always will be the experience of a collective psyche which needs to mark and give meaning to the passage of time. The glory of the Catholic liturgy is that it has always beautifully done this. The symbols are all there. What we have to do is keep them from degenerating into empty shells."

According to the Constitution on the Sacred Liturgy (no. 102), it is by celebrating the liturgical year that the faithful lay hold of the mysteries of redemption and "are filled with saving grace." But what is the precise relationship between our celebration of these mysteries and our sanctification? How are we filled with saving grace? This question is probed by Patrick Regan in "Liturgical Year: Source of Spirituality." Abbot Regan describes how liturgical spirituality, especially that nurtured by the regular cycle of feasts and seasons, begins with the Exodus of Israel, culminates in the sacrifice of Jesus, and is extended in history through sacraments and feasts. A feast, he says, is a memorial "of divine revelation and human sanctification." Through festal celebrations we are led to the very center of the process of sanctification; our lives are drawn into the time of the kingdom, and we open ourselves to transformation by the presence of the Risen Lord among us.

The recent reform of the liturgical calendar has challenged us to reevaluate the relationship between the religious and the civil calendars. Does there exist, as some would claim, a tension between the two? In "Liturgical Year: Conflict and Challenge," Sr. Kathleen Hughes examines this relationship by utilizing Niebuhr's categories describing the relationship between Christianity and culture: opposition, identification, purification, paradox, and transformation. It is "transformation," says Sister Kathleen, which best expresses the relationship between religious and secular feasts. Although there may at times be diametrical opposition between the two, transformation "is that mode of relationship which takes the Incarnation seriously . . . which urges us to seek always to discover and to release those human rhythms and cultural idioms which may serve as a vehicle for transformation into Christ." Faithful to this view of the relationship between the liturgical and civil years is the method Sister Kathleen calls "dialogical liturgical renewal." Applying this method, she surfaces a number of issues to be considered

as we reflect on the future of the liturgical year. Sister concludes with several remarks indicating areas for further
research and discussion on the liturgical year in general,
Sunday, and feast days.

The Federation of Diocesan Liturgical Commissions is
grateful to The Liturgical Press for making these addresses
available in published form

> Lawrence J. Johnson
> Executive Secretary
> Federation of Diocesan Liturgical Commissions

Sunday: The Heart of the Liturgical Year

MARK SEARLE

It needs to be said at the very outset that the liturgical year is more than a calendar: it is a carousel of sayings and stories, songs and prayers, processions and silences, images and visions, symbols and rituals, feasts and fasts in which the mysterious ways of God are not merely presented but experienced, not merely perused but lived through. The challenge confronting us, then, is not so much historical or theological or catechetical. The challenge is to address ourselves to the liturgical year and its various facets on its own terms, the terms in which image, symbol, and ritual come to us, the terms of the imagination. It addresses itself first and foremost to the imagination, drawing that imagination deeper and deeper into the redemptive mystery of Christ.[1]

There are several reasons why Sunday deserves to be called "the heart of the liturgical year." As the oldest element of the Christian calendar, it is the nucleus around and out of which the feasts and seasons of the year have evolved, and still it retains in itself the kernel of the whole Christian mystery. Historically, it is the original Christian feast. Theologically, it encapsulates the whole economy of salvation. Pastorally, it is the day when the local Church

13

comes to realize itself as Church and when all the faithful are called to find themselves within the whole story of God. For better or worse, therefore, our experience of Sunday will largely condition the way we imagine our Christian life: as something freeing or as a burden of obligation resentfully borne; as life with a God in whom we may delight, or as life with a God of whom we would rather be free. Our attitudes towards God, Church, and world derive less from our thoughts about them than from the way we imagine them; and the experience of Sunday, I would suggest, is a major source of ambivalent feelings and attitudes.

One corollary of this is that it is worthwhile, from a pastoral point of view, to pay close attention to people's actual experience of Sunday, both in their childhood and now, and to their experience of Sunday as a whole. For some, childhood memories of Sunday are memories of boredom and frustration, of a day that was one long yawn. For others there are memories of the sounds and smells of church, of family dinners and excursions. We all have our own selective memories of Sundays when we were growing up, and so do the people we serve.

We also have our present experiences of Sundays, both positive and negative. For many Sunday is still a day for gathering family and visiting friends; for others it is a day when they often have to work; for others it is a day for sleeping late, reading the papers, and generally lounging around. Going to church may or may not be a regular part of what Sunday means to people.[2] Still, it is to that larger experience of Sunday, to those habits of mind and to those unexamined expectations, that we must address when we speak of Sunday as the heart of the liturgical year. Even for those who go to church, churchgoing is only part of what that day means: it also may mean a day of work, or a day when you can't buy beer, or a day for going out to the mall. And in this larger context, one last thing is worth noting, namely, that professional church workers have a very specific experience of Sunday as a busy day, a day of work, a day spent in church and with crowds of people. Such an experience, we need to be reminded, is neither typical nor, it must be said, ideal. In other words, our own pattern of Sunday living may not be a very good starting place for preaching the mystery of Sunday to others.

It is not my purpose here, however, to examine the various images of Sunday that may exist in our culture and among our people. I simply want to draw your attention to the fact that such images do exist and that they have an impact upon how Christians imagine their total religious lives. I would like, instead, to work with some images of Sunday found in our tradition and to develop them in such a way as to draw out their implications for the whole Christian life. So I shall be understanding my assignment—to speak of Sunday as the heart of the liturgical year—as an invitation to make sense of the claim that images of Sunday are also images of Christian life and life-style. I would like to begin with some reflections on Sunday as sabbath and Sunday as a day of resurrection. Then I shall touch briefly on a couple of other secondary images of Sunday before trying to develop a new image of Sunday which is true to the tradition and yet strong enough to generate new insights and, perhaps, new patterns of living.

IMAGES OF SUNDAY

1. *Sunday as sabbath.* Many of us grew up with an understanding of Sunday which was profoundly colored by its being tied to the third commandment of the

Decalogue: "Thou shalt keep holy the sabbath day," such sanctification being accomplished by hearing Mass and abstaining from servile work. Now the link between Sunday and sabbath is very complex, but the image of Sunday which sees it as the fulfillment of the third commandment suffers two serious drawbacks. First, it is a rather late development, probably not earlier than the sixth century. Second, and this is not unconnected with the fact that Sunday was only interpreted as fulfilling the sabbath obligation at a time of pastoral decline, it is a legalistic understanding of the role of Sunday in the Christian life: it sees it as an obligation, not as a pathway of the Spirit.

In large part this legalistic approach to Sunday, itself based on a legalistic understanding of the Torah in general and the Decalogue in particular, represents a misinterpretation of the role of the sabbath in Jewish life and so complicates the problem of understanding the relationship of sabbath to Christianity. Western legalism and a reading of the Jewish law heavily colored by New Testament polemics against some contemporary interpretations of its force and meaning, current among certain Christian groups, has left us with an impoverished image of the Jewish sabbath, which only something like Abraham Heschel's book *The Sabbath*[3] can help us overcome. Essentially, the Jewish sabbath derives its vitality from two sets of images found in the ancient texts of Exodus and Deuteronomy:

> Remember the sabbath day, to keep it holy.
> Six days you shall labor, and do all your work;
> but the seventh day is a sabbath to the Lord your God;
> in it you shall not do any work,
> you, or your son, or your daughter . . .
> or the sojourner who is within your gates;
> for in six days the Lord made heaven and earth,
> the sea, and all that is in them,

and rested the seventh day;
therefore the Lord blessed the sabbath day
and hallowed it (Exod 20:8–11).

And in Deut 5:12–15 we read:

Observe the sabbath day, to keep it holy,
as the Lord your God commanded you.
Six days you shall labor, and do all your work;
but the seventh day is a sabbath to the Lord your God;
in it you shall not do any work,
you, or your son, or your daughter,
or your manservant, or your maidservant,
or your ox, or your ass, or any of your cattle,
or the sojourner who is within your gates,
that your manservant and your maidservant may rest
  as well as you.
You shall remember that you were a servant in the land
  of Egypt,
and the Lord your God brought you out thence
with a mighty hand and an outstretched arm;
therefore the Lord your God commanded you to keep the
  sabbath day.

Theories about the origin of the sabbath and the history of these texts need not detain us here.[4] What is important for our purposes is that these two sets of images of the sabbath link it with the creation story and the Exodus. The link with creation associates the rhythm of work and rest with the primordial creativity of God and with his delight in creation. Work leads to rest, rather than rest being for the sake of work, and resting from labor is something which both hallows or glorifies God and sanctifies people through their imitation of God. Imitation of God is also involved in the liberation motif: freedom is a supreme value, the foundational gift of God to Israel, to be enjoyed not only by those who have the wealth to enjoy the luxury of leisure but also by those who work for them.

Such was the idea and the ideal of the sabbath. But,

as we know all too well, religious visions have a tendency to be reduced to definable obligations, so that the conflicts between Jesus and the Pharisees over sabbath observance are best understood less as an attack on the sabbath as such than as an attack on a narrow legalism which had distorted people's perception of this great gift of God. Ironically, the Christian tradition mainly took over this legalistic understanding of the sabbath, first in rejecting it and then later, in the sixth century, in reappropriating it and applying it to the Christian Sunday.[5] But Jesus himself was neither purifying the sabbath law nor destroying it. Rather, he seems to be proclaiming that the sabbath represented a vision whose time had come. The "rest" of God and the definitive liberation from slavery to work have arrived in the messianic age, present in the person and work of Jesus. The new age, which he inaugurated by his death and resurrection, has a sabbatical character and is properly understood as a new creation and a new exodus in which we are all invited to share.

We shall pick up those themes again later, but it is worthwhile to ask the question of whether the Christian Sunday can be properly understood through a catechesis which takes as its starting point the third commandment. Surely it would be better to start with the new works of creation and liberation wrought by God in Christ and to work back to the sabbath, rather than by starting with a legalistic distortion of the sabbath and trying to fit the Christian Sunday into that narrow framework. There is absolutely no evidence to suggest that the early Church saw Sunday as a Christian sabbath. There is some evidence to suggest that some Christian groups considered the law of sabbath observance to be binding on Christians as well as Jews,[6] so that both Saturday and Sunday were highly significant days. But the consensus that generally came to prevail in the early decades of the Church is that what the sabbath represented had actually been realized in the whole new age ushered in by Christ, of which the first day of the week became the symbol.

Moreover, it should be noted that the first day of the week was a day for assembling to worship; never, among Christians, a day for abstaining from work. Christians were to exercise their new-won freedom and celebrate the "rest" of God after the new creation by their total life-style, seven days a week.

Thus it is misleading to speak of Sunday in terms of sabbath observance, yet it is essential to speak of the Christian era—and thus of Sunday which symbolizes it—in terms of the two-fold imagery of the sabbath: sharing in the "rest" of God and enjoying, and extending to others, the freedom God has won for us. Thus, while rejecting the idea that we are still obliged by the Old Testament legislation on the sabbath—whether that is understood as applying to Saturday or to Sunday, Christians can nevertheless identify with and appropriate most of the spirituality of the sabbath, such as it is developed by Abraham Heschel. But it will be applied not just to one day of the week but to the Christian life as such.

2. *Sunday as day of resurrection.* In apostolic times Christians began to meet together on the first day of the week. So much was this weekly assembly (*ekklesia*) a part of their lives that it came to identify them, whether they continued to frequent the sabbath synagogue or not.

It is commonly said that Sunday developed as a Christian assembly-day for two reasons: once the sabbath was over, Christians could gather for their own assembly on Saturday evenings (which, in Jewish reckoning, marked the beginning of the first day of the week). This Saturday evening gathering lasted until early Sunday morning, the time of Christ's resurrection. Consequently, regular Sunday assembly became an integral part of early Christian life for reasons both of convenience and symbolism.

A major difficulty with this thesis, however, is that the earliest evidence seems to suggest that Christians met not on Saturday night and Sunday morning, but on Sunday evening.[7] Only in the second century, perhaps, was there a general shift in the meeting-time from Sunday evening after work to Sunday morning before work. Moreover, there is no explicit attempt to relate the weekly assembly to Christ's resurrection early in the morning on the first day of the week until the late second century. Thus, while the tradition of linking Sunday observance with the resurrection of Jesus is ancient and valid, it is important to remember that it is not the original understanding of Sunday and could be misleading.

It is more likely, as I have said, that the original time for assembly was Sunday evening. Why Sunday evening? Perhaps it has something to do with the fact that, in Luke and John at least, the encounters of the disciples with the Risen Lord occurred on the evening of the first day of the week. Recent scholarship has tended to place more emphasis on the encounters with the Risen One and to see the accounts of the empty tomb as secondary.[8] It also underlines the fact that there are no descriptions of the resurrection of Jesus, only of encounters with Jesus after his resurrection from the dead. The focus, then, is not on the resurrection itself, but on encountering the Christ. This is significant since it takes our attention off questions of how the resurrection took place and points us to look at the resurrection of Jesus as first and foremost a datum of the experience of the disciples. Similarly, the fact that they gathered regularly on a Sunday evening—the time of encounter, and not on Sunday morning—the putative time of resurrection, suggests that the Sunday evening assembly was understood not as a commemoration of the fact of Jesus' resurrection but as the context and occasion in which they would meet him again. Notice how, in Luke and John, it is in the course of a common meal that Jesus appears to them. And, of course, in Acts, Peter makes the amazing claim that "[we] were chosen by God as witnesses, who ate and drank with him [Jesus] after he rose from the dead" (10:41).

This would seem the original and best starting point for talking about Sunday observance: Jesus' manifestation of himself to his disciples at table in the evening of the first day of the week. Incidentally, it is also the proper starting point for talking about resurrection and Eucharist, not to mention Church. So Eucharistic catechesis would best start with the resurrection meals rather than the Last Supper. Sunday is best spoken of in the context of ecclesiology, and ecclesiology is best spoken of in terms of being witnesses to the power and Spirit of God who raised Jesus to victory over death. The reason for this is straightforward enough. When God raised Jesus from the dead, a new age dawned in the history of humanity. Indeed, a new humanity came into being as a result of some people's shared exposure to the Risen Christ and shared experience of his Spirit operative in their own lives. Resurrection gives rise to Church in the context of the Eucharist.

That is why baptism came to be restricted to Sunday, and especially to Easter Sunday: the neophytes undergo the death and resurrection experience of the disciples, and in the same way, namely, through encountering the Risen Lord. The restoration of adult initiation at Easter gives us the chance to understand the events of the first Easter, to see that Christianity is fundamentally a new way of living in time, a new *modus vivendi* deriving from their participation in the death of Christ and from the encounter with him at table when they too eat and drink with him after his rising from the dead.

3. *Other images of Sunday.* The various names given to the Christian Sunday—the Lord's Day, the first day of the week, the eighth day, the day of resurrection—all serve to cluster groups of images which invite us into the mystery of Christian life itself.

To speak of Sunday as the first day of the week, for example, is to use terminology obviously derived, as is the seven-day week itself, from Judaism. In biblical tradition it is the first day of creation, the day when light was created and darkness rolled back from the face of the earth. Now, in Christ, God has undertaken a new work of creation in which he once again proves victorious over the darkness. A vivid awareness of the cosmic significance of Christ's redemptive work eventually permitted Christians to adopt the pagan usage of referring to this day as the day of the sun, using the metaphor of dawn to speak of the Christian era as representing a new and unending day for all humanity. But notice again how the understanding of the day, Sunday, derives from how we understand the historical period in which we now live. The day is not a commemoration of the resurrection, but a symbol or sacrament of our whole experience of time.

The image of the eighth day bespeaks the same reality. As the eighth day of a seven-day week, Sunday is the sacrament of a new relationship to time which transcends the weekly rounds of work and recreation. We are invited to live in a qualitatively different kind of time. It is to that kind of time that I would now like to turn, reflecting in the light of these historical notes upon what Sunday means to our sense of time as Christians. In this, I am returning to some ideas I have developed elsewhere.[9]

SUNDAY AS TIME OF LIFE-AFTER-DEATH

In his *Little Book of Eternal Wisdom,* Henry Suso, the fourteenth-century German mystic, relates a dialog with Eternal Wisdom.

> THE SERVANT: Lord, what wilt thou teach me?
> Reply of ETERNAL WISDOM:
> 1. I will teach thee how to die;
> 2. and I will teach thee how to live;
> 3. I will teach thee to receive Me lovingly;
> 4. and I will teach thee to praise Me fervently . . . .
> THE SERVANT: . . . . Lord, dost Thou mean a spiritual death, which Thy dolorous death has so lovingly demonstrated, or a bodily death?
> Reply of ETERNAL WISDOM: I mean both of them.
> THE SERVANT: Lord, why should I need to be taught about bodily death? It teaches itself well enough when it comes.
> Reply of ETERNAL WISDOM: If anyone postpones the teaching until then, he will be lost.
> THE SERVANT: Alas, Lord, it is still somewhat painful to me to hear about death. [10]

Someone once quipped that the real question is not whether there is a life after death, but whether there is a life before death. Clearly, there are different ways of thinking about death, and each colors the way we think about life before death and life after death. I would like to mention briefly three ways of thinking about the relationship of life to death.

1. An obvious way to think about death is to think of it as the termination of life, as a parting from all the things of life. John Dunne writes about this view of death in his book *Time and Myth.* There he describes "the things of life" in terms borrowed from the Book of Ecclesiastes: "There is a season for everything and a time for every purpose under heaven." He continues:

The things that are named by Koheleth are all the seasonal activities of man: being born and dying, planting and uprooting, killing and healing, tearing down and building up, weeping and laughing, mourning and dancing, scattering and gathering, embracing and holding apart, keeping and casting away, rending and sewing, keeping silence and speaking, loving and hating, making war and making peace. Each of them has its time.

And John Dunne comments: "If there is a life in man that can survive death, it is none of these."[11]

Because the life that survives death cannot be identified with any of these activities that make up life, Christians have been ambivalent about them, seeing them often as distractions from the life of the world to come. Certain kinds of other-worldly Christianity preach the greatest possible detachment from these things of life, since death is the end of them. Death is the point of discontinuity, the termination of life, which is feared by the wicked and looked forward to by the pious.

2. Our own culture shares this supposition that death is the termination of life, but elects to ignore it as far as possible. It is probably not unfair to say that our culture is characterized by its forgetfulness of death: death is taboo. We can afford to ignore death because our common life is dominated, not so much by individuals who must die, but by collective processes which go on indefinitely. Collective processes transcend the comings and goings of individual participants and can thus survive the death of the individual. They operate independently of the human cycle of birth and death. They have a life of their own, a life into which we are constantly exhorted to throw ourselves. We enter such collective life, dedicate our energies to it and then fall away, to be replaced by others. We die, yet life goes on.

Because of this, ours is a death-defying culture; but it is worth pondering what this denial of death does to the people who participate in it, yet must themselves die.

In the first place it is worth noting that this collective life consists precisely of the things for which there is a season and the purposes for which there is a time. It is an endless succession of working, acquiring, using, and disposing; of producing goods and services to create wealth which is then channeled back into the system by our use and consumption. It is a life where every goal is but the means to attaining some further goal: consumption is for the sake of production which is for the sake of consumption; work pays for the leisure which refreshes us for work.

Life in our society is defined in terms of this process. To throw oneself into life is to cease to live an autonomous, personal existence in order to become part of the process. It means living an existence which is not only dominated by impersonal, collective processes, but which is also itself reduced to an object of exchange. The impersonal forces of production and the impersonal statistics of consumption have the effect of rendering us, in our turn, impersonal units of productivity and consumption. Our value is derived from our role as producers and consumers. As this happens, we ourselves become subject to the same criteria of usefulness and expendability to which we have learned to subject other things and other people.

Thus the very cycle which defies death by surviving our passing is at the same time the treadmill of our servitude. We become subservient to the processes of our society, define ourselves in their terms as producers and consumers, lose any sense of our God-given dignity and vocation. In the death-defying processes into which we are co-opted for our life-span, we are identified by our role, not by our name. These processes are necessarily anonymous:

the name dies, the role goes on. Conversely, it is confrontation with death which makes us aware of the unique value of our personal lives, of our inescapable individuality. If "soul" is the name we give to the principle whereby we relate to our own unique identity and destiny, then our society, in calling us to throw ourselves into this collective life, is literally soul-destroying. Under the illusion of suiting our own purposes in life, we become in fact admirably suited to the purposes of the system, mere workers and purchasers who fade in and out of the remorseless economic process. In such a context it is clear that the three-day weekend has nothing to do with the Christian Sunday: it is merely the time when the phase of production yields to the phase of consumption. "If there is a life in man that can survive death, it is none of these."

3. But there is another way of conceiving death in its relationship to life, and that is to see death as an event within life itself. The paradox of Christianity is that we are a people who have confronted death and survived it. "You have been taught that when we were baptized in Christ Jesus we were baptized in his death . . . we went into the tomb with him and joined him in death . . ." (Rom 6:3–4). In the Letter to the Colossians, we are challenged with the question: "If you have really died with Christ to the principles of this world, why do you still let rules dictate to you, as though you were still living in the world?" (2:20-21). We have seen what it means to be living in this world, subject to its impersonal principles of production and consumption, earning and spending. But what would it mean to live with death behind us? What would it mean to be already living life-after-death, the life of the world to come?

One of the most interesting sections of Raymund Moody's famous *Life After Death* (1976) is that in which he recounts the effects of near-death experiences on those who survived them. Moody remarks:

> There is a remarkable agreement in the "lessons," as it were, which have been brought back from these close encounters with death. Almost everyone has stressed the importance in this life of trying to cultivate love for others, love of a unique and profound kind. One man who met the being of light felt totally loved and accepted, even while his whole life was displayed in a panorama for the being to see. He felt that the question that the being was asking of him was whether he was able to love others in the same way. He now feels that it is his commission on earth to try to learn to be able to do so.[12]

Moody characterizes the effects of close encounters with death by speaking of life being "broadened and deepened," realizations of the shallowness of previous lives and life-styles, changed attitudes to the body, to the present moment, to the life of the mind, to one's relationships with others.

I am not in a position to comment on the validity of such claims and I do not wish to raise them to the status of a theological argument, but one cannot help being struck by the parallels with the kind of outlook and life-style advocated by the New Testament writings. Would it be altogether outrageous to claim that the New Testament was written *by* those who had been through death *for* those who had been through death? In any case it is clear that a close encounter with death—and the same can probably be said of any profound crisis which disrupts the normal pattern of life—has two important effects. First, it has the power to engage us inescapably as persons: nothing is so lonely as death, nothing so calculated to confront us with the truth of who we are. Second, such an experience has the effect of rendering all our other engagements relatively unimportant: what seemed to matter so much ceases to matter at all; people and things that had gone unnoticed and unappreciated now seem newly dear and precious, as if seen for the first time. Such an experience has the effect, as it were, of pulling us out of the gravitational pull of the world's atmosphere, to the point where we can see life as a gift and relate to it and to all that enters into it with greater simplicity and clarity.

To come back from the dead, then, would be to see people and things, not as objects to be used for our own purposes, but as they are in themselves. It would be to know the truth of things instead of being blinded by our own projects and preconceptions. Instead of producing in order to consume and consuming in order to produce, it would be to follow the advice of Bhagavadgita, "Act without seeking the fruits of action." In other words, if you build a house, be attentive to the house itself, not to the price you hope it will fetch. When you serve a client, let it be for the sake of the client, not for the wage. When you cook, let it be for the sake of the food, not just for eating. When you eat, let it be with grateful appreciation, not just ingesting to provide energy for something else. When you plant, let it be with respect for the seed and the soil, not just with an eye to the harvest. When you dance, let it be for the dance, not for display. . . . In other words, whereas those who live life-before-death live in a world of using and being used, those who live already the life of the world to come are those who have learned to relate personally to the things of life and to the people they encounter. They know the difference between serving God and serving mammon and that the service of God is perfect freedom.

The effect of sharing in the death of Christ is perfect freedom: freedom from the tyranny of collective principles, release from the treadmill of doing and getting. It opens our eyes to the fact that it is who we are, not what we have or produce, that will survive death. As John Dunne puts it, "The things that come to an end in death are all the things that have their proper time and season in life. Spirit is not one of these, but is rather man's relationship to each and all of them."[13] Baptismal death is entry into the life of the Spirit, the life of being free and setting free. To us who have died it is given to transform the relationships that constitute our world, to renew the face of the earth.

Thus the baptismal themes of new creation, liberation from slavery, through participation in the death and resurrection of Jesus and being sealed with his Spirit, are precisely those which our tradition has associated with Sunday. Clearly Sunday differs radically from the three-day weekend. The three-day weekend belongs to the old order, to the system wherein life is defined as earning and spending. Sunday also differs from the sabbath. Whereas the sabbath is a day of rest from labor, a momentary participation in the rest of God which preceded creation and will follow history, Sunday represents the altogether more radical idea that the life of the world to come is already here. It lasts, not twenty-four hours, but from the resurrection of Christ unto ages of ages. Sunday is the eighth day, shattering the treadmill of the seven-day week, celebrating the incursion of life-after-death into the lives and history of the human race.

Sunday also differs from the sabbath in that it is chiefly our day of assembly. Unlike the sabbath, it is not a day which is holy in itself, but a day on which Christians, whose every day is holy because they live the life-after-death, emerge from the camouflage of lives lived quietly in an unbelieving world and are seen for what they are: the firstfruits of the age to come, the beginning of a new humanity set free from anonymous, impersonal, death-denying processes, to serve the living God.

Bram Stoker's novel *Dracula* features the "undead." These are the unfortunates whose blood has been sucked by the beast. Their spirit is dead, but their bodies continue to function: they are helplessly driven to seek the blood of others, reducing them, too, to the dreary existence of the "undead." They are people in need of redemption, but their only hope is to be allowed to die. We who have been allowed to die in baptism have been redeemed from the world of the undead: we might style ourselves, to continue the metaphor, "the grateful dead." Sunday is the day when we gather to celebrate our redemption with Eucharistic thanksgiving, giving thanks for the death of the Lord and for our own death also, through which we have been born to a new and everlasting life.

It is in this context of grateful appropriation of the new life-beyond-death won for us by Christ that the second dimension of the so-called Sunday obligation is properly to be considered. For it would render our Eucharistic thanksgiving hollow if we were not, in fact, a people set free from servile work.

The concept of servile work has an interesting history. In classical antiquity the term "servile work" was used in contrast to the "liberal arts" to refer to the kind of drudgery which is required if life is to keep going. In this sense servile work not only included the labor of slaves and other menials, but also the more "intellectual" occupations of people such as scribes. In contrast, the liberal arts represented those occupations which required creativity and imagination, or which, in other terms, enhanced the quality of life. Early Christian writers, and especially St. Augustine, took up the distinction as one which covered the whole of Christian life: servile work, they claimed, was work carried out in servitude to Satan, the work of sin. [14]

Both of these concepts of servile work have something in common to what we have described as life-before-death, life subject to the principles of production and consumption. Thus abstention from servile work cannot be understood as merely time off from work, or as time for going shopping, or as time to be spent on mind-drugging "pastimes." Abstention from servile work has to be conceived positively as the reclamation of our God-given freedom from the collective processes, whether they be those of production or consumption. This will mean, certainly, taking time for recreation of mind and body, but it means even more than that. Abstention from servile work means developing a life-style that is liberal and not servile, a demonstration of freedom rather than unthinking submission to social and psychological compulsions. As such, it prompts us to explore simpler and more frugal life-styles; to foster friendships; to live reflective lives, both personally and communally. It impels us to discover the secrets of practicing contemplation in a world of action. In this way the rediscovery of the meaning of Sunday will necessarily be associated with the development of a counter-cultural Christian life-style, in which such traditional Sunday practices as reading and prayer, family gatherings and visits to friends, care for the sick, the dependent, the imprisoned and the stranger, will link up with contemporary concerns about the quality of life, about the pollution of our environment, about consumerism and about violence. In all these different ways, it seems to me, we not only keep the sabbath holy, but we begin to bring about a sabbatical for an earth that is exploited and polluted and for a people that is wearily enslaved to noise, work, consumption, and violence.

CONCLUSIONS

1. It is important to recognize how profoundly our sense of ourselves is derived from those with whom we live and interact. Our sense of identity is derived largely from participation in our communities, but community is a matter of shared imagination: a common way of understanding the world and our own place in it. Sunday, I have argued, exists to shape the Christian imagination, but it is suffering unfair competition from all the images of self and society which exist in our culture and which owe nothing to the gospel. So we need to ask: what sort of collective imagination do our Sunday practices create and foster?

This question would apply right across the board, from the number of Masses celebrated on Sunday and the pace at which they are conducted, to the implicit expectations which are communicated concerning how people spend the rest of the day. It is important to remind ourselves again, however, that the laity generally have a very different experience of Sunday from that of the clergy and their associates. [15] For clergy and church workers Sunday is seen as the high point of the week, the culmination of so much other effort. For most lay people, however, it is less the culmination than the source of the week's enterprises, a time of nourishment and refreshment. If Roman Catholic levels of church-attendance have dropped off rather sharply over the past twenty years, this may well have something to do with the widespread dissatisfaction registered by the laity with regard to preaching. Satisfaction with preaching declined from 44 per cent fifteen years ago to a miserable 20 per cent today, which would seem to suggest that the majority of Catholics who still come to Mass no longer find it a source of strength and nourishment. [16]

We need to recognize the importance of the imagination as a source of belief, moral behavior, and even personal identity. Instead of didactic, moralizing or even entertaining preaching, we need a rich diet of scriptural, traditional, and contemporary imagery, imagery which can help us discover our Christian identity and become acutely aware of the difference between life lived before death and life lived after death, between the life of the good pagan and the radical newness of life lived in Christ.

2. The "Sunday Mass obligation" is a contradiction in terms. Christ died to set us free, so that the Christian life is essentially an exercise in freedom, a freedom which is not license but which is exercised in the Spirit as a result of encountering the Risen Christ. A third-century Syrian document, the *Didascalia*, speaks of the Sunday assembly in these terms:

> When you are teaching, command and exhort the people to be faithful to the assembly of the church. Let them not fail to attend, but let them gather faithfully together. Let no one deprive the church by staying away: by so doing they deprive the Body of Christ of one of its members. . . . Do not, then, make light of your own selves, do not deprive the Body of Christ of his members; do not rend, do not scatter, his Body.[17]

Note here the appeal to the Christian imagination concerning the identity of the Church and the individual's place within it. The result is quite a different sense of the Christian economy and of one's place within it than that communicated by talk of "Sunday obligation" and "pain of mortal sin."

3. Though it probably does more harm than good to talk about Sunday in terms of keeping holy the sabbath day, the theme of Sunday rest and its roots in the Jewish sabbath are not to be neglected. The two themes, or sets

of images, associated with the Hebrew sabbath have now passed over into the new age as characterizing the life-style of those who have passed from death to life. The image of the Christian people and its world as a new creation must prompt us to ask what the difference is between a baptized life and an unbaptized life and what it means already to share in the "rest" of God. Similarly, the Exodus imagery encourages us to recognize our own freedom and to set others free: your son and your daughter, your manservant and your maidservant, your ox and your ass. But what would it mean in practice to be free of the enslavements of the "undead"? What would it mean to relate to one's family, one's employees, one's employers, one's possessions—even to strangers and enemies—as people who have been liberated? How would this affect our relationships to such things as our work, our leisure, money, status, our use of authority, our emotional and affective life? How are these things experienced as enslaving? How would liberated people relate to them?

4. What are we to do about those who have been baptized but have never really died to be raised to new life in Christ? What are we to do about those who are still the slaves of their unredeemed imaginations?

In the first place we have to discover our own freedom and exercise it gratefully. Much pastoral ministry appears to spring, not from encounter with the Risen Lord, but from the principles of this world: from fear of the consequences of allowing people to be free, from unthinking acceptance of the principles of sociology and psychology, from secular concepts of what education, maturity, and so on are all about. Some pastoral ministers appear more comfortable erecting buildings or establishing programs than they do speaking of Christ. But the fact of the matter is that if we cannot say, "We have seen the Lord: he is truly risen," our ministerial identity is derived from some other source and we are probably imposing some other gospel.

On the other hand, if we have met the Lord—and the New Testament suggests there are all sorts of situations in which that can happen, then we shall have a transformed imagination. If we have a transformed imagination, we shall allow others their freedom: we shall not attempt to impose our theology or our ethics on them or attempt to tell them what to do. We shall rather appeal to their imagination, as Jesus did in speaking to them in parables. If such an approach succeeds in challenging and transforming their imagination (and Jesus himself found that it did not always succeed), then the Church will happen without our building it, Christian morality will follow without our legislating it, Christian belief will follow without our having to argue its reasonableness.

The New Testament, I have suggested, is best understood as a collection of writings written by the dead for the dead, the death of which we are speaking is that which occurs in going into the tomb. There, in the tomb, we encounter the power of God to give life to the dead. Without that experience of death and of being raised from the dead, Christian beliefs and Christian morality either make no sense at all, or are merely overlaid upon an imagination which remains untransformed. Sunday, with its assembly, its preaching, its breaking of bread, is essentially a post-resurrection appearance of the Risen Christ in which he breathes his Spirit upon his disciples for the forgiveness of sins and for the life of the world. As such, it is the point at which all the central images of the Christian life converge and, because the liturgical year is but the spinning out of these images from week to week, the Christian Sunday may properly be claimed as the heart, not only of the liturgical year, but of the Christian life itself.

NOTES

1. On the importance of imagination for liturgy, see Patrick Collins, *More Than Meets the Eye* (New York: Paulist Press, 1983).

2. See William R. McCready, "The Role of Sunday in American Society: Has It Changed?" in *Sunday Morning: A Time for Worship*, ed. M. Searle (Collegeville: The Liturgical Press, 1982) 97–120.

3. Abraham Heschel, *The Sabbath* (New York: Farrar, Strauss & Giroux, 1951).

4. The reader is referred to Roland de Vaux, *Ancient Israel: Its Life and Institutions* (New York: McGraw-Hill, 1961) 475–83; Thierry Maertens, *A Feast in Honor of Yahweh* (Notre Dame: Fides, 1965) 152–92; and W. Rordorf, *Sunday* (London: S.C.M., 1968) 45–54.

5. Rordorf, *Sunday* 171.

6. For a recent study of the diversity of Christian attitudes towards the Law in apostolic times, see Raymond Brown and John P. Meier, *Antioch and Rome: New Testament Cradles of Catholic Christianity* (New York: Paulist Press, 1983) esp. 1–9.

7. Rordorf, *Sunday* 193–237. "We are, therefore, almost compelled to conclude that there was a direct connection between these (post-resurrection) meals on the one hand and the breaking of bread on the other. There does exist, then, good reason for supposing that in the primitive community the breaking of bread, for which no definite date is mentioned in Acts 2:42, 46, took place weekly on Sunday evening" (pp. 236–37).

8. For example, A. Stock, "Resurrection Appearances and the Disciples' Faith," *Bible Today* XX (1982) 2–4, 90–96.

9. "The Shape of the Future: A Liturgist's Vision," in Searle, *Sunday Morning: A Time for Worship* 129–53.

10. *Little Book of Eternal Wisdom and Little Book of Truth*, trans. and with an introduction by J. M. Clarke (New York: Harper & Brothers, n.d.) 126–27.

11. John Dunne, *Time and Myth* (Notre Dame: University of Notre Dame Press, 1973) 12.

12. R. Moody, *Life After Death* (Harrisburg: Stackton Books, 1976) 88.

13. Dunne, *Time and Myth* 13.

14. References given by Rordorf, *Sunday* 103, n. 1 and 104, n. 3.

15. See McCready, "The Role of Sunday . . ." 112–14.

16. *Ibid.* 112.

17. English translation from Lucien Deiss, *Springtime of the Liturgy* (Collegeville: The Liturgical Press, 1979) 176–77.

Liturgical Year:
What Does It Mean to Remember?

TAD GUZIE

Since our topic is remembering, bear with me while I do some remembering of my own, and a little bit of theological history related to our topic. A quarter of a century ago, when I first got interested in liturgical theory, the name Odo Casel seemed to appear in every book or article that I read on liturgy. Casel was a German Benedictine who attracted the attention of the theological community during the 1920s. His major effort was to explain how the mystery of Christ is made present in the liturgical action.

The theology of Casel's day explained the "presence of the mystery" in terms that came out of scholastic philosophy: it is the effects or fruits of the saving act of Christ which are made present in the action of worship. Casel felt that this view diminished the reality of Christ's presence. The central idea in his theory was that Christ's saving act itself is made present in the liturgical celebration, not merely the grace which Christ won for us. The liturgy therefore involves an "objective re-presentation" of the redemptive act of Christ, and Casel marshaled a host of patristic texts to support his thesis. His critics, reading the same texts, insisted (for example) that liturgical re-presentation is not "objective" but rather "effective."

And so the debate went on. As it goes with most theological controversies, no one said the last word. The debate simply petered out, largely because it centered around the language of scholastic philosophy and the nuances of terms like "objective" and "effective" and "representation."

I will not bore you with the details of the *Mysteriengegenwart* controversy. But I had to mention it because, as I worked on this topic assigned to me, I was continually aware that I was dealing with the same question that Casel struggled with fifty years ago. "Remembering," in its liturgical sense, has to do with the *Mysteriengegenwart*, the presence of the mystery of Christ. However, fifty years after Casel, we no longer deal with liturgical questions in the essential categories of scholastic philosophy. Today our approach is more existential, more rooted in the concrete experience of ritual. Our language is more phenomenological than metaphysical. It is less abstract and more descriptive.

In this paper I will try to set the human experience of "remembering" before your mind's eye and describe it from many sides. In the end I hope that you will hear nothing you don't already know. I would simply like to *engage you in the activity of remembering* and get you to reflect on it as we go along.

But before we begin, I feel obliged to mention the gratitude we owe to scholars like Odo Casel. Half a century ago there was simply no liturgical theology worthy of the name. Theologians talked about how Christ is substantially present in the Eucharist and how the Mass renews the sacrifice of Calvary. But the liturgical action which took place at Mass was seen as a *mere ritual setting* which, apart from "confecting the Eucharist," did little more than subjectively recall events that happened long ago. Casel was among the first to push us beyond the mentality which saw the sacraments in terms of words of consecration or matter and form. He saw that the *whole liturgical celebration* is a fully "realizing" symbolic activity and that the liturgy makes the mystery of Jesus present to us in a much larger way than what the theology of matter and form could conceive. In contemporary terms Casel saw that the whole liturgical action is an act of "remembering," and this act is much more than a matter of recalling the historical past.

Since Casel's time we have developed a whole biblical theology of "anamnesis" to back up the idea that remembering makes something present. Times change, theories change. *Mysteriengegenwart* gives way to *anamnesis*, and somehow we never finish with the business of reflecting on what it means to celebrate and remember. But theological analysis is usually too far removed from everyday life. Theology tends to move into sacred talk and hieratic language before it has taken a thorough look at ordinary human experience. I think this is true of our liturgical talk, which gets eloquent about "celebrating the Paschal Mystery of Christ" before we have said enough about the radical mystery of human existence.

So I would like to frame the question of what it means to "remember" in a larger context than that of the Christian liturgy. Let's look at the kind of "remembering" we do at the sort of celebration which we usually consider nonreligious, ordinary, and everyday.

A family gathers for a reunion. What happens at this event? As the folks mingle and reacquaint themselves with one another, stories are told. The stories are "small change," simply old stories, pieces from the past. Remember when Uncle Charlie's toupee got caught in the Christmas tree? Or when Cousin Mary, who never drinks, got a little high and wouldn't stop singing that song about Mockingbird Hill? If you are a new member of this family, say through marriage, you either enjoy the stories because you have begun to identify with the family, or you feel alienated because you don't feel close enough to what is going on. Stories, in fact, are the bond that holds the group together. (Scholars tell us that most of the stories told in the Old and New Testaments were remembered, and eventually written down, because the Hebrews and the early Christians gathered for reunions and told what they remembered.)

But the storytelling at a family reunion is only part of the picture. Remembering is a natural invitation to festivity, and so it goes at our reunion. The same songs are sung, the same games are played. The food is served on the same best china, with the same best candlesticks on the table. People like ritual and familiar actions, and that is why we do them over and over. We don't feel compelled to change the words of "Happy Birthday" from year to year. (Creative liturgy does not mean ever new texts. The familiar words of the liturgy, such as the words of the Eucharistic Prayer, serve a whole function which is nonintellectual and nonconceptual.)

In the example of the family reunion, we find the two elements which theoreticians find at the heart of ritual in any culture. First, there is a remembering, a retelling of the group's common story. Second, there is play or dance or a symbolic action like a shared meal, which pulls the whole event together. (The liturgy of the Word and the liturgy of the Eucharist, storytelling and shared meal, combine to form quite an archetypal ritual.)

Let us reflect on some questions: in the course of any year, what festive events (religious or otherwise) are most important for you? What are you remembering, and why

are these events festive for you? I have asked these questions in many groups, and the answers that people gave
jibed with the scenario which I have just outlined. The
yearly events that meant the most to them were those where
a common story was shared, savored, and enjoyed and
where there was a festive action, like a special Mass or a
special meal, which they could count on to involve
everyone. Genuine remembrance and genuine celebration
go hand in hand. You can't find the one without the other.

At this point I should distinguish *remembering* from
reminiscing. "Reminiscing" pertains to recalling events
from the past, simply and utterly as past events. There are
people who seem to live entirely in the past and who
reminisce because the present is empty for them. But I don't
think this is the norm. Even people who appear to live in
the past tell their stories because there is some "ought" or
"should" which they want their listener to hear. For most
people the main reason for recalling events from the past
is that the past affects us in some way in the *present.* This
is what I would call "remembering" in distinction to pure
"reminiscing."

Reminiscing at a family reunion is fun, but we don't
tell the stories about Uncle Charlie or Cousin Mary out
of pure historical interest. Our storytelling brings to life
the whole image of our family identity. That is why we
go away from the reunion with a sense of refreshment, or
at least realization: this is who we are, for good or for ill,
as a family. And new members of the family are saying
within themselves: "I can't stand it" or "I really love this."
Such reactions would not be possible if "remembering" did
not have something subtly profound to do with the *present.*

To sum up, remembering and celebrating go hand in
hand. Celebration in fact is the natural context for
remembering. Remembering is not pure reminiscence or

recalling the past for its own sake; the past is recalled because it affects the present. The past *is* present, and that is why we are celebrating here and now. But remembrance and celebration are not ends in themselves. Celebration is a time-out from the pace of everyday life, a breathing space which gives us time to remember who we are. A good celebration returns us to everyday life with new eyes, a fresh awareness of ourselves, and sometimes even a new sense of purpose. Here we arrive at an idea which is not usually associated with the popular meaning of "remembering": *remembering leads us into tomorrow and inserts us into the future.*

In short, when it is done in the context of celebration, remembering is a symbolic activity which joins the three dimensions of time: past, present, and future.

This is starting to get a bit heady and metaphysical. Let me try to say the same thing in more descriptive language. Remembering means *seeing my personal story in relation to a larger story*. This is what happens (or is meant to happen) at a family reunion, an anniversary or a birthday celebration, or the Sunday liturgy. We live in the midst of larger stories than our own personal stories. We grow up with the larger stories of our family, the communities that surround us, our religious tradition, our nation, and finally our whole culture. The purpose of remembering is to plug us into the larger stories that surround us and impinge upon our lives. Remembering gives us a past and a future. It helps us to sort out the meaning of our personal stories, and in so doing it leads us into what might be a more meaningful future.

This is why Christians celebrate the Lord's Day. We do so because hearing the Word, breaking the bread and sharing the cup, pull us out of our private experience, our individual stories, and invite us to enter the story of Jesus.

Think of the Eucharistic Liturgy as one large act of "remembering." There are two parts to the action. The technical theological terms are Word and sacrament. The more experiential terms are *story-telling* and *meal-sharing*. The liturgy of the Word is the time when we tell the "family story" in the hope of entering into it more fully and illuminating our own personal histories. The liturgy of the Table is another way of remembering who we are: one bread, one body in the Lord who easters in us each time we break the bread and share the cup.

This is the theory of what our Sunday liturgy is about. Our actual practice is a different story, which I will not belabor here, because you all know the distance we have to travel in making our liturgical books come alive. Let me turn now to the subject of the liturgical year.

Liturgical renewal after Vatican II has affected the celebration of Advent and Lent in most parishes, and much has been done to restore the celebration of the Easter triduum to its rightful place. But we have only made a beginning. This past Lent I happened to be working with a group of sixty religious educators who represented an entire province of Canada. Our task was to spend a few days reflecting on the RCIA and its implications for religious education in Catholic schools. At one point I asked the group how many of them, in their home parishes, had adult catechumens who were preparing for baptism. The answer: less than a quarter. This meant that over three-quarters of a random selection of parishes were not yet involved in that process which I think is essential if we are not to remain a "filling-station" Church. Or perhaps I should turn the statistic around and feel happy that nearly a quarter of the parishes represented by these people have taken some steps to reach out to the unchurched.

Unless there is an active catechumenate and unless there

are candidates seeking initiation into the Catholic Christian community of *this* parish, the liturgy of Lent which is celebrated in *this* parish is likely to be abstract and theoretical. The lectionary and the liturgy of Lent are all about baptismal renewal, but real live catechumens are an essential symbol to the rest of the community: they concretize and embody what the baptismal life is all about. A parish without catechumens is bound to have a Lenten liturgy without "guts."

But how many of our parishes can say that they really have something to offer to the unchurched folk who are all around us? The RCIA does refurnish the celebration of Lent and Easter, but this is not because of rites and liturgy alone. It is the *reaching out* to people who are not members of our community that makes final sense of our paschal celebration.

Another problem related to the liturgical year is that many of our pastoral practices violate what the liturgy preaches. The timing of infant baptism is still based on when a baby is born, not when the Christian community celebrates the great baptismal feasts. The time of confirmation is still based on the bishop's schedule. In the great majority of places in North America, we seem to baptize and confirm at almost any time of the year indiscriminately—even during Lent. Under discussion now in various dioceses is the promoting of the full observance of the "fifty days of Easter" and bringing all of our initiatory practices into line with what we preach about the Paschal Mystery. This is a very substantive matter, with pastoral implications that would change the face of the liturgical year as we now observe it. It deserves serious attention.

Lent and Easter and the fifty days of Easter are the heart of the Christian year, and enough can never be said about their importance. But let's broaden our scope and look at the rest of the year. We have to face the fact that the liturgical calendar does not square with the rhythm of celebration that most people live. I recall reading that around a century ago the American Catholic bishops were asked to approve a Mass text for the feast of Thanksgiving. They declined, on the grounds that Thanksgiving was not a Catholic feast but one with Protestant origins. We have come a long way since those defensive days, but this example illustrates a problem that is still very much with us: the Church's official liturgy has paid little attention to the rhythm of celebration that North Americans have adopted.

Let's look for a moment at the secular calendar of feasts. In using the term *secular*, I am not implying an opposition between the sacred and the secular, the holy and the profane. I simply mean the non-liturgical calendar of holidays which North Americans in general tend to observe. The days in my list are those of which people are inclined to say, "We try to do something special in the family that day."

There is an interesting rhythm to the secular calendar: Days of celebration tend to come along every four to six weeks. For example, Thanksgiving is followed a month later by the high holidays of Christmas. (In the United States, doesn't the *real* Advent begin as soon as the long Thanksgiving weekend is over?) At the end of January, we begin to see the hearts and flowers advertising Valentine's Day. For many people this mid-February feast marks the middle and perhaps the worst of winter. If you missed Valentine's Day, you might be pretty desperate by March 17, that day on which everyone becomes Irish.

In the secular calendar Easter is a celebration of lilies and the coming of spring. It is followed in the secular calendar not by Pentecost but by Mother's Day and, a month later, Father's Day. Civil religion then celebrates its major feast on the Fourth of July. (Canada does this on July 1, with a bit less flourish and fewer fireworks.) The secular calendar provides nothing else until Labor Day, undoubtedly because people are taking their own time-out and finding space for celebration during their vacations. In any case the Labor Day weekend is the occasion for a great many cookouts because it marks the end of summer vacations for adults and children alike. During the next six weeks, the trees turn gold and red and then they are bare. Halloween comes along, marking the end of fall and the beginning of winter.

Individual families work birthdays and anniversaries into their calendar of festivities as well. So feel free to revise my list of feasts in accord with the experience of your own family or community. However you revise it, I think you will come up with the same general *rhythm* of a feast every four to six weeks, with longer spaces during the summer vacation period.

The secular calendar is certainly a motley assortment of feasts. Some are religious in origin, some are not. Some seem to be excuses for a party at dull times of the year, like St. Patrick's Day at the grey and slushy end of winter, or Halloween at the barren end of fall. (Halloween is also that one time in the year when we get to act out some of our fear of death and fantasies related to the dark side of the world of spirit.) Some feasts in the secular calendar are very family-oriented, like Mother's Day and Father's Day, and so religion pays them attention. (Have you ever heard of a homily on the second Sunday of May which did not manage to link mother with the readings of the day?)

We can take a cynical approach to the secular calendar and say that Madison Avenue is behind most of these holidays. Advertising certainly promotes the buying and giving of gifts, but I don't think it creates the occasions for gift-giving. The secular calendar of feasts is a product of our collective psyche. It came into being for reasons that are as natural as our biological functions. First, it marks the passage of time with special moments and thus addresses an innate human need. Second, the secular calendar is an open-ended invitation to take time out for celebration, another innate human need.

But what are we supposed to be celebrating? To celebrate means to remember, and as I tried to emphasize above, the act of "remembering" involves us in the future as well as the past. One feast in the secular calendar has a very explicit future dimension: The Fourth of July is the occasion (at least in the media) for much reflection on where we are going as a nation. But for the most part, our secular feasts are oriented toward remembrance of the past. Mother's Day and Halloween and Labor Day are little concerned with inserting us into the future.

What about the Christian liturgical year? Let's look for a moment at the sanctoral cycle. This cycle of the liturgy celebrates our history, our heritage, indeed the "communion of saints." In itself the sanctoral cycle is more oriented toward the past than toward the future, and this is legitimate enough. There is a time for remembering the past. Members of religious communities usually relate strongly to the feasts of their founders and other canonized members of their community. But the calendar of saints is heavy on clerics and religious, and there is little for lay Christians to "remember" in any way that relates to their own lives and experience. The revision of the calendar of saints after Vatican II cleaned up the universal Church calendar by weeding out long-forgotten or purely local personalities. This did not address a far more basic problem related to the sanctoral cycle.

The difficulty with institutionalized liturgy is that it always seems to be too late. By the time it canonizes or holds up to our "perpetual memory" an event or a person who was extremely significant for a decade or a generation, the whole story has begun to fade. The Christian people, of course, have long since learned to go their own way. They remember, they commemorate, they celebrate what is important to them. That is the way the calendar of saints came into being. But the names inscribed in that calendar have always belonged to a place and a time, a community and an era. And if the official liturgy moves at a snail's pace in changing a few words in the Eucharistic Prayer, it is even slower to recognize the relevance of events and people with whom Bob and Carol and Ted and Alice out there in the pews might identify.

I doubt that the sanctoral cycle of the liturgy can be made to speak to most Catholics of late-twentieth-century North America until it includes a commemoration of the martyrdom of Martin Luther King, or of Archbishop Romero and the four women who were murdered in El Salvador. "Remembering" in its best liturgical sense has to do with the living past as well as the distant past. Given its particular nature, the official calendar of saints does not incite much "remembering" in the full liturgical sense that we have been discussing. Still, any parish can become more sensitive to the persons and events that people *do* want to remember. (Couldn't we get the publishers of those liturgical desk calendars that lie on every pastor's desk to add people and events from the living past? A good many "secular" calendars do.)

The sanctoral side of the liturgical year has difficulty in rising above remembrance of the past and relating to the *present*. Let us now look at the seasonal portion of the liturgical year. Here, I think, Christian liturgy shares some

of the same difficulties which we saw in the secular calendar of feasts, where the biggest problem is relating to the
future.

The future dimension of "remembering" seems to have
been unusually strong in the first decades after the death
of Jesus. The weekly Day of the Lord was the only Christian feast. This was the day when the faithful met for worship, strongly aware that in breaking bread in memory of
the Risen Lord they were looking forward to the final day
when the new creation would be realized. The expectation of an imminent Second Coming had waned before the
end of the first century, and Christians had a sense that
the temporal world was not likely to disappear next week
or next month. But it still took quite a while before they
began to mark the passage of time with feasts and seasons.
It is not until the second century A.D. that we see signs of
a feast of Easter, that is, a time of the year which com-
memorated the historical event of Jesus' death and resurrection. For a good long while the liturgical cycle was based
on the week, not on the year.

Four centuries later the picture looked quite different.
Sunday retained its importance, of course, but there was
now a fully developed cycle of feasts and seasons com-
memorating the events recounted in the New Testament.
By the fifth century, in other words, the *historical past* had
acquired an importance which it did not have for earlier
Christians.

Scholars have evaluated this development in different
ways. To some, it appears that Christians merely accom-
modated themselves to the time and the place, taking over
and "baptizing" the old pagan feasts of sun-gods and
nature-gods. It is certainly undeniable that Christians
picked up the old feasts, the old "markers" of the passage
of time, and reinterpreted them in accord with their own

religious experience. The ancient Hebrews had taken over fertility rites and nature feasts in the same way. What the Hebrews had done with Mesopotamian and Canaanite culture, Christians eventually did with the Greco-Roman culture. I remember one liturgical scholar saying that the evolution of a liturgical year was an astonishing development because, for Christians, *every* celebration of the Eucharist is a celebration of the life, death, and resurrection of Jesus. I would argue to the contrary. Whatever we say about the meaning of the individual Eucharist, we still need a larger psychic calendar to mark the passage of time. So it would have been astonishing if Christianity had *not* eventually restructured the time of the year and given its own distinctive meaning to the passage of time.

Still, Christianity is not a cyclical religion. Every Eucharist proclaims the death of the Lord "until he comes again," and this is a reminder that we are radically oriented toward the future. If this theme of expectation and hope is forgotten, the liturgical cycle will draw us into an eternal repetition of events which, however meaningful and comforting they may be, really lead us nowhere. In primitive religions, if Eliade is right, the cyclical reenactment of sacred dramas made the "terror of history" tolerable. The regularity of sacred feasts and seasons enabled the people to put up with the terrifying irregularities of nature, misfortune, and injustice.

Cyclical religion is not dead. It is kept very much alive by people for whom religion and worship consecrate the status quo, the search for the good life, people who are disturbed by anything which upsets the present order of things. Many church-goers are quite content with the present and the past. At Christmas we think of how nice it is that there was at least one peaceful event in history. We think of how nice it would be if there were more of the spirit of this beautiful season in the world, this season of good cheer and twenty-four-hour cease-fires. At Easter we are reassured that Christ came out of the tomb, that spring is coming, that the lilies still bloom. Period. In this perspective the past reassures us and makes the present tolerable. As for the future, there will always be another Christmas, another Easter, an endless cycle to comfort us and give meaning to the passage of time, while we go on living pretty much as we always have.

What does it mean to remember? I have tried to sound out some of the dimensions of this profoundly human and sacred activity. I have talked about family reunions, the celebration of birthdays, the secular calendar of feasts, the Sunday Eucharist, and the liturgical year—all of these in one long breath. That is the way it has to be, because the activity of "remembering" transcends all of our categories about sacred and secular, holy and profane. If you have ambiguities about the difference between a family reunion and the Sunday Eucharist, this is a healthy ambiguity. It will push you beyond thinking about the Eucharist in terms of words of consecration, or who says what and when. "What does it mean to remember?" is a question that cuts through a great deal of the magic that has surrounded Catholic practices.

The liturgical calendar, like every calendar, is and always will be the expression of a collective psyche which needs to mark and give meaning to the passage of time. The glory of Catholic liturgy is that it has always beautifully done this. The symbols are all there. What we have to do is keep them from degenerating into empty shells. If we are true to the gospel, the portion of time that we need most to mark and to remember is the future. This implies a liturgy which is oriented always to conversion, change of heart, and constant revision of our assumptions about the way we are and the way we ought to be. We are still learning how to enact such liturgy.

Liturgical Year:
Source of Spirituality

PATRICK REGAN, O.S.B.

To give some context to our topic, let me mention that the founders of the liturgical movement understood the liturgy in no other way but as a spirituality. In the mid-nineteenth century when Dom Guéranger called the faithful back to the official worship of the Church, he asked them, "Where would you obtain the spirit of prayer if not at its natural source?"[1]

At the beginning of this century, Pius X declared in his famous *motu proprio* on sacred music that "active participation in the holy mysteries and in the public and solemn prayer of the Church is the primary and indispensable source of the true Christian spirit."[2]

By 1914 the role of liturgical prayer in Christian life had become a matter of heated debate. Lambert Beauduin took his stand in *La Piété de l'Eglise,* later translated by Virgil Michel and published under the title of *Liturgy: The Life of the Church.* We might render it today as *Liturgy: The Spirituality of the Church.* The author portrayed Catholics of his day as isolated individuals left to find their own way to God. Many had abandoned the practice of prayer altogether or else had drifted into devotional exercises owing more to fantasy than to sound doctrine.

53

Religion was disconnected from social and political realities and confined to the inner realm of subjective consciousness, thus furthering the schemes of those bent upon emancipating humanity entirely from God. Finally, the hierarchy conducted itself as a vast administrative bureaucracy or police force, not as an organ of spiritual paternity generating divine life and calling forth filial trust from the faithful.

Beauduin summoned the Church to nourish these famished souls with the rich fare of her own spirituality, the liturgy. He based his plea on three propositions: 1) Jesus Christ, High Priest of the new covenant, is the unique source of supernatural life. If others are to share this life, they must be united with his person. 2) Christ exercises his sanctifying power only through a hierarchical priesthood. This priesthood is operative in the Church through the sensible signs which comprise the liturgy. The liturgy, then, is the full expansion into the Church of Christ's own priesthood. 3) Union with this hierarchy in the very exercise of its priesthood is for every Christian the authentic mode of union with Jesus Christ and therefore is the primary and indispensable source of supernatural life. [3] In this argument the remarks of Pius X in 1903 began to find their theological underpinning.

In the first issue of *Orate Fratres*, which appeared in 1926, Virgil Michel expressed his hope that "many persons may find in the liturgy the first answer to the intimate need of their souls for a closer contact and union with the spiritual and the divine." [4]

Although the Constitution on the Liturgy issued by the Second Vatican Council admitted that "the spiritual life is not confined to participation in the liturgy," [5] it declared unambiguously that "the liturgy is the outstanding means by which the faithful can express in their lives, and manifest to others the mystery of Christ and the real nature of the true Church";[6] that it "builds up those within the Church into . . . a spiritual dwelling for God";[7] that it is "the summit toward which the activity of the Church is directed and the fountain from which all her power flows."[8] And yet in the early 1970s, at the very moment when the reformed rites were being implemented, we saw the sudden explosion throughout our country of programs and institutes of spirituality! Their proliferation and success suggest that people are now finding in them what the liturgy promised but has not yet delivered.

Many reasons can be offered for this phenomenon. Perhaps the pioneers were naive in their expectations of what changes in our patterns of worship could accomplish. Perhaps the changes themselves turned our attention from God and so preoccupied us with the publication of books, the search for vernacular music, the training of ministerial personnel, rearrangements of space and furniture, and the quest for social relevancy and psychological plausibility, that those seeking a deep experience of prayer decided to look elsewhere. Perhaps the performance level in most communities is still so low that the discriminating prefer to risk the dark night of the soul rather than endure another Sunday of the "Ode to Joy" sung to a computer organ. On the other hand, since the spiritual life is not exhausted by participation in the liturgy, perhaps the interest in spirituality should be seen as a complement to liturgical renewal, or even the fulfillment of it, rather than as a threat. In any case these considerations make the topic assigned to this meeting both important and timely.

SPIRITUALITY

Spirituality is a slippery term having many meanings. In its broadest sense it designates a path to holiness, a way of establishing, fostering, and verifying our relationship with God. It includes methods to be employed in this endeavor as well as thematization of the content and implications of the experience. Simply put, it is the entire process of sanctification: God revealing, calling, and giving himself; human beings discerning his voice, responding, and being transformed as a result. This relationship between God and his people is celebrated at the liturgy. Composed of words and gestures which are publicly posited and capable of repeated enactment, the liturgy gives full ecclesial actualization to the encounter with God and articulates its official meaning. It also shapes our subjective awareness of the relationship and directs us now to live accordingly. Hence the liturgy is rightly called the Church's normative method of spiritual growth.

Obviously our relationship with God exists prior to its ritualization and perdures after it. Indeed it can be cultivated, examined, and restored by personal prayer, reflective reading, spiritual direction, solitude, fasting, and other acts of asceticism. For this reason the spiritual life is not restricted to participation in the liturgy. But neither is it restricted to what lies outside the liturgy. Unfortunately spirituality is sometimes understood in just this way: a methodical course aimed at intensifying union with God, but with no attention to the ecclesial actualization of this union in public worship. In this view liturgical activity may still be considered important and necessary as a channel of grace, but it falls outside the scope of spirituality. History, of course, attests many forms and schools of spirituality which focus and thematize the path to God in basically non-liturgical terms. This is regrettable, but true. When it occurs, advocates of liturgy and advocates of spirituality are set in opposition and compete with each other not only for diocesan funds and registrants in degree programs but even for the allegiance of the soul.

I do not intend to pursue this debate any further or attempt to resolve the tension. My purpose is to set forth the nature and characteristics of a spirituality nurtured at its normative source, the liturgy, with particular concern for the celebration of feasts and seasons.

A spirituality shaped by the liturgy is characteristically biblical, paschal, ecclesial, and transformational. It understands the process of sanctification—of being freed from sin and made holy through union with God—as historically rooted in the event of redemption: begun in the Exodus of Israel, completed in the pasch of Jesus, and extended in time through the sacraments and feasts of the Church.

SANCTIFICATION BEGINS WITH THE EXODUS OF ISRAEL

The process of sanctification begins with Israel's redemption, the goal of which is the creation of a holy people. To redeem means to deliver, to release, to set free. We find these words applied to Israel's Exodus. The Lord said to Moses: "I will free you from the forced labor of the Egyptians and will deliver you from their slavery. I will rescue you by my outstretched arm" . . . (Exod 6:6). But deliverance is only half the meaning of redemption. The other half is acquisition, ownership, coming into possession. The Lord not only said, "I will free you from the Egyptians"; he added: "I will take you as my own people, and you shall have me as your God" (Exod 6:7). The Exodus from Egypt necessarily leads to Mount Sinai, where God offers a covenant to the people he redeemed: "If you hearken to my voice and keep my covenant, you shall be my special possession . . . . You shall be to me a kingdom of priests, a holy nation" (Exod 19:5–6). Redemption is ordered to sanctification: to the formation of a holy people, a people set apart from others and belonging to God.

We recall, though, that Israel's special relationship to its Redeemer was violated as soon as it was initiated. The covenant and the golden calf were made at one and the same time. The enduring reality of sin made Israel's keeping of the covenant impossible and adultery inevitable. So the Lord spoke through the prophet Jeremiah:

> The days are coming . . . when I will make a new covenant with the house of Israel and the house of Judah. It will not be like the covenant I made with their fathers . . . for they broke my covenant . . . . But this is the covenant which I will make . . . . I will place my law within them, and write it on their hearts. I will be their God, and they shall be my people. . . . for I will forgive their evildoing and remember their sin no more (Jer 31:31–34).

Jesus, on the night he was betrayed, took the cup—the cup of blessing that was the memory of the passage from Egypt and the covenant of Sinai—and said: "This cup is the new covenant in my blood. Do this . . . in remembrance of me" (1 Cor 11:25). Jesus identifies the shedding of his blood as the inauguration of the new covenant promised through Jeremiah, the covenant which will never be broken because it is always kept by Jesus. And because it is always kept, forgiveness and sanctity are assured indefinitely. In the death and glorification of Jesus, then, redemption reaches fulfillment. Humanity is delivered from sin, is sanctified, and made the definitive possession of God.

SANCTIFICATION CULMINATES IN THE SACRIFICE OF JESUS

Since the time of the prophets, the Hebrews were aware of the existence of sin—their tendency to refuse God's gifts, to go their own way, to turn their backs to him instead of their faces. They devised elaborate rituals to expiate wrongdoing and secure lasting union with God. But none of them were effective. Year after year on the Day of Atonement the high priest would go beyond the veil of the sanctuary into the Holy of Holies, the dwelling place of God. Within the Holy of Holies was the ark of the covenant, the throne upon which the divine presence rested. The high priest would sprinkle it with the blood of sacrificed animals and burn incense before it, praying for forgiveness and mercy (Lev 16:1–28). And each year he would come out from behind the veil to discover things to be just the way they were before he went in, even as Moses, coming down from the mountain, tablets in hand, discovered the golden calf.

The Letter to the Hebrews draws a sharp contrast between these futile expiatory rituals and the enduring efficacy of Christ's sacrifice. Its teaching on the priesthood of Christ was expounded by all the pioneers of the liturgical movement and is the basis for Vatican II's statement that "the liturgy is considered as an exercise of the priestly office of Jesus Christ. In the liturgy the sanctification of man is manifested by signs perceptible to the senses . . . . Every liturgical celebration, because it is an action of Christ the priest and of his Body the Church, is a sacred action surpassing all others."[9]

As explained in the Letter to the Hebrews (chapter 9), the high priest of old went behind the veil of a tent on earth. Christ ascended to highest heaven, the true place of God's presence.

The high priest of old entered the Holy of Holies year after year, and necessarily so since none of the sacrifices he offered ever took away sin. Their multiplicity testifies only to their ineffectiveness. Christ offered a single sacrifice and is now at rest, his work completed once and for all. The covenant which he inaugurates is both new and eternal.

Upon the lid of the ark, the high priest of old sprinkled the blood of animals, attempting to placate God by sacrifices extrinsic to himself. Upon the wood of the cross, Christ shed his own blood, surrendered his very self, and so abolished sin where it resides: within the human heart and not outside of it. By pouring out his Spirit into our hearts, he purifies our inner selves from dead actions so that we can serve the living God by our own living.

The high priest of old went behind the veil and stood before the throne alone. The rest of Israel was confined to the other side of the veil. Their sanctification always remained incomplete because no sacrifice ever brought them within to the presence of God. Instead it always left them exactly where they had been before the sacrifice: outside and unaffected. But Christ our high priest has placed his Spirit within us, uniting us with himself both in his sacrifice for sin and in his ascent to heaven. The veil separating God and his people is now torn in two from top to bottom (Mark 15:38), and we are summoned to approach with confidence the throne of mercy to receive grace and favor in time of need (Heb 4:16). In the Spirit-filled Christ we ourselves have become the temple, the priesthood, and the sacrifice. As Peter tells us in his First Letter: You are "living stones, built as an edifice of spirit, into a holy priesthood, offering spiritual sacrifices acceptable to God through Jesus Christ" (2:5). The promise made at Sinai is realized in us, for Peter adds: "You are a chosen race, a royal priesthood . . . a people he [God] claims for his own . . ." (2:9).

Finally, when the high priest of old had finished his ministry, he himself had to leave the sanctuary and return to the other side of the veil. His contact with God was momentary. He had to go back to his former condition and deal once again with the sin he still shared with the rest of his people. Nothing had changed. Christ, however, has ascended to heaven and has never come back. Purified of the sin which he took upon himself for our sake, his humanity is now totally transformed and made a new creation. He is permanently enthroned at God's right hand, communing with him unceasingly. He continually intercedes with the Father on our behalf and, in the power of his Spirit, lifts us up to heavenly places to have fellowship with him and all who belong to him. Everything has changed. When the high priest of the new covenant returns from behind the veil and appears a second time, it will not be to deal with sin but to bring salvation to those who await him (Heb 9:28). Paul makes the same point to the Colossians: "Since you have been raised up in company with Christ, set your heart on what pertains to higher realms where Christ is seated at God's right hand. . . . After all, you have died! Your life is hidden now with Christ in God. When Christ our life appears, then you shall appear with him in glory" (3:1–4).

SANCTIFICATION IS EXTENDED IN HISTORY THROUGH SACRAMENTS AND FEASTS

As we have seen, the process of sanctification is the transformation of the innermost core of our humanity from being sinful to being holy, from being estranged to God to being united with him, from being dead to being regenerated and made to live a new and different life. This transformation, begun in the call of Israel, was finally accomplished in the humanity of Jesus. He freely took our sin, our rebellion, our estrangement from God upon himself. And by his death, put them to death, because his death was the culminating moment of a life-long surrender to God. Having abolished sin by his death, he opened his humanity out to the Spirit of holiness who fills it with God's own life and reveals him, raised from the dead, to be Son of God, only-begotten of the Father.

Sanctity is inseparable from Christ. It is not an object which can be detached from him and parcelled out to others individually and successively. If that were so, each of us would be sanctified one at a time and one after the other—by the merits of Christ certainly, but not in union with him. We would still be an assortment of individuals, each one holy, but still apart from each other and apart from Christ. We would not yet be a holy people, and for that reason we would still be estranged, still in sin. Sanctity is inseparable from Christ. It is his person, himself— not as a static entity, but himself in the very act of sanctifying, himself in the very act of dying and being raised to life; himself in the very act of abolishing sin and being filled with the Spirit of holiness, in virtue of which he is, as man, Son of God. If we are to be sanctified, therefore, we must be united with the person of Christ in his own act of sanctification. He must carry us into his own death and glorification; into his own freedom from sin, into his own holiness, into his own condition as Son of the Father and Temple of the Spirit.

How does this come about? Through faith? Yes. Not a faith that merely admits that Jesus existed, or even that he died and rose; but rather a faith that also confesses that in his dying the Spirit who raised him to life is poured out *through* him to be the source of my own life (Rom 8:11). This is a faith that moves me to die with him so as to live with him. This is a faith that leads to baptism. Christ didn't die *instead* of us, so that we wouldn't have to. He died *for* us, so that we could die with him, and in dying with him live with him. The only death which leads to life is his, no other, and certainly not our own apart from him.

But in baptism we join him in his death (Rom 6:3), or rather he draws us into his own dying. And we emerge partakers all together of his one new life, his one sanctified humanity: a holy people, a communion of saints.

Spiritual life begins in baptism, for it is nothing less than life in the Spirit of Christ. It is nourished at the Eucharistic table. There the Spirit moves us to prayer. We give thanks and praise to the Father for his power. We remember everything he did to make us one and holy: everything from the creation of the world to the glorification of Jesus. And we ask him to send his Spirit upon the bread and the cup to make them the Body and Blood of Christ, so that we who share them together may become one body, one spirit in Christ—an everlasting gift to the Father, the definitive manifestation of his sanctifying power.

Through the Eucharist of the Church, the once for all death and resurrection of Jesus are extended into the ongoing movement of history, sanctifying it and claiming it for God and his purpose. Successive moments of time are brought together into the fullness of time, the time of Christ, the time when he bursts the gates of hell and enters upon unending life. Thus the time and space of this world are transformed into the place of God's rule and made to reveal him as Lord.

Let me now add a few comments about the role of feasts. The sweep of salvation history, summarized in the baptismal creed and Eucharistic anamnesis, is spread throughout the year in the form of feasts and seasons. The great events whereby God brings us to new life in the Spirit of his Christ are thereby inserted into the temporal structure of the world itself. Hence feasts and seasons represent the memorial as well as the present availability of the events they commemorate. As the Lord told our ancestors on the night of their deliverance: "This day shall be a memorial feast for you, which all your generations shall celebrate with pilgrimage to the Lord, as a perpetual institution" (Exod 12:14).

The same can be said of any feast. It is a perpetual memorial in time of divine revelation and human sanctification, which we forget only at our own peril. The annual return of holy days summons us to remember and appropriate in yet another year a relationship with God which is eternally valid. In this way we preserve continuity with our past, acquire meaning for our present, and obtain direction for our future.

Christian spirituality does not derive from an arcane gnostic myth or an abstract sapiential system which considers spiritual life to be incompatible with temporal life. It derives from one who was born when Quirinus was governor of Syria, whose way was prepared by the preaching of John in the fifteenth year of the rule of Tiberius Caesar, who suffered under Pontius Pilate during the feast of Unleavened Bread, who was taken up to heaven forty days later, and whose Spirit was poured out in Jerusalem on the fiftieth day, Pentecost. These events of sanctification happened in specific moments of time. Yet they are relevant to all time. And so we continue to celebrate them at specific moments so as to transform our own time into the time of salvation, which in Christ is always Now (2 Cor 6:2) and Today (Heb 3:7—4:11).

Seen in this way the celebration of feasts is one of the primary ways in which the Christian mystery is incarnated and inculturated. The more important the feast, the more ancient, universal, and constant is its observance. Hence the feasts themselves, properly celebrated, draw us to the center of the process of sanctification and prevent us from drifting to the periphery. Furthermore, the distribution of the various events of salvation throughout the year requires every Christian to face them every year. No one can ignore the economy of sanctification in its temporal unfolding except by ignoring the feasts. Our subjective attachment to the various feasts and our manner of celebrating them thus serve as an excellent measure of the quality and breadth of our spiritual life.

Since the Eucharist makes present the total mystery of Christ, it might be objected that the remembrance of particular events on particular days is unnecessary or even detrimental. Human psychology, however, argues to the contrary. Tertullian and other third-century writers knew this with regard to the prayer of the hours. Whatever is supposed to be remembered and done at all times, risks being remembered and done at no time unless it is prescribed for at least some time. To take a somewhat trivial example, all of us are supposed to show gratitude for our mothers' love on all days. But the observance of Mother's Day assures that we do so on at least one day. The same dynamic seems to underlie the growth of feasts in the Church.

Once established, the holy day gathers together an extremely rich assortment of biblical, doctrinal, moral, and devotional themes, and gives them a particularly vivid temporal focus. The *Magnificat* antiphon of Christmas vespers is the most daring: "On this day Christ is born, on this day the Savior appeared, on this day the just rejoice and sing: 'Glory to God in the highest.'" The *Exultet* is more lyrical: "This is the night when first you saved our fathers; this is the night when Jesus Christ broke the chains of death and rose triumphant from the grave." Historically, of course, they're wrong. December 25 is not the actual day of Jesus' birth. And Easter Sunday is not the night of the Jewish pasch. But liturgically they're absolutely correct, for the feast makes present the event it celebrates.[10]

Each feast generates endlessly new expressions of the mystery in the form of antiphons, hymns, sermons, and icons, which nourish spiritual life for centuries and which would not exist if it were not for the feast. These in turn serve as means of access to the inexhaustible content of the mystery celebrated. For this reason prayerful reflection on the materials of the feast is indispensable for fruitful celebration. This was easier for previous generations, thanks to Dom Guéranger[11] and Pius Parsch.[12] Adrian Nocent's four volumes[13] don't quite do it for the present generation. Nor is religious education and systematic theology helping. Their presentation of the faith often owes more to humanistic psychology or speculative philosophy than to the biblical, liturgical, and patristic tradition. Hence they do not lead students naturally to the place where faith is celebrated.

To conclude let me point out that the significance of feasts for Christian existence is nowhere illustrated more graphically than in the opening action of the paschal vigil. The priest traces the first and last letters of the Greek alphabet as well as the current year on the paschal candle. As he does so he proclaims: "Christ yesterday and today, the beginning and the end, Alpha and Omega; all time belongs to him and all the ages." The paschal Christ is the Alpha and Omega of creation; the one through whom and from whom all things live (Rom 11:36; Col 1:16; Heb 1:2). By inscribing the current year on the candle, the community inserts its fleeting moment of history into the enduring presence of "the First and the Last and the One who lives. . . . forever and ever . . ." (Rev 1:17–18). Isn't this what all feasts do? By annually celebrating them the faithful of any given time and place open themselves to the source and goal of life. Though they sojourn in a world which comes to be and passes away, they are confident that in Jesus Christ risen from the dead they already abide in eternal life.

NOTES

1. Prosper Guéranger, *The Liturgical Year*, trans. Laurence Shepherd, 15 vols. (London: Burns, Oates, and Washbourne, 1931) I, 5.

2. Pius X, "Tra le sollecitudini: The Restoration of Church Music." A full translation of the paragraph from which this sentence is taken is given as follows in James J. Megivern, ed., *Worship and Liturgy* (Wilmington: McGrath Publishing, 1978), no. 28: "It being our ardent desire to see the true Christian spirit restored in every respect and be preserved by all the faithful, we deem it necessary to provide before all else for the sanctity and dignity of the temple, in which the faithful assemble for the object of acquiring this spirit from its foremost and indispensable fount, which is the active participation in the holy mysteries and in the public and solemn prayer of the Church."

3. Lambert Beauduin, "Le Piété de l'Eglise," in *Mélanges liturgiques* (Louvain: Abbaye du Mont Cesar, 1954) 11.

4. Virgil Michel, *Orate Frates* I (1926) 2.

5. *Constitution on the Sacred Liturgy*, no. 12, in Walter M. Abbott, ed., *The Documents of Vatican II* (New York: Guild Press, 1966) 143.

6. *Ibid.*, no. 13, in Abbott 13.

7. *Ibid.*

8. *Ibid.*, no. 10, in Abbott, 142.

9. *Ibid.*, no. 7, in Abbott, 141.

10. "Recalling thus the mysteries of redemption, the Church opens to all the faithful the riches of her Lord's powers and merits, so that *these are in some way made present* at all times, and the faithful are enabled to lay hold of them and become filled with saving grace." *Constitution on the Sacred Liturgy*, no. 102, in Abbott, 168 (emphasis mine).

11. See note 1.

12. Pius Parsch, *The Church's Year of Grace*, trans. William G. Heidt, 5 vols. (Collegeville: The Liturgical Press, 1957).

13. Adrian Nocent, *The Liturgical Year*, trans. Matthew J. O'Connell, 4 vols. (Collegeville: The Liturgical Press, 1977).

Liturgical Year:
Conflict and Challenge

KATHLEEN HUGHES, R.S.C.J.

The title of this paper, "Liturgical Year: Conflict and Challenge," takes a position about the relationship of the liturgical and civil calendars. Whether a particular event is regarded as a conflict and a challenge is a choice of language predicated on a prior judgment about the relationship of the liturgical and secular years and, indeed, about the existence of sacred and secular time.

To speak, for example, of the coincidence of June 17, 1984 of Trinity Sunday and Father's Day as a conflict is to have determined that the liturgical year is under siege, at least some of the time, from its civil or secular counterpart. As I began to think about this topic, that was a judgment I was not willing to adopt without a little investigation. (Surely, in the case of the intersection of Trinity Sunday and Father's Day, the community might be spared a lot of dubious theology if the homilist's remarks were limited to fathers.) I am suggesting that there could be many relationships between the liturgical and the civil year such as, and to continue the alliteration: crisis, cooperation, conundrum, convergence, communion, collision, consonance, claim, connection, etc.

69

The first task before us is a brief exploration of the several possible relationships that might exist between these two calendars. Second, I propose that we are faced at this moment with some serious pastoral anomalies when we compare the ideal of the liturgical year as specified in the Constitution on the Sacred Liturgy and later documents and pronouncements and the reality of the average Christian's experience of the year. In this instance we ignore contemporary experience to our peril. I will therefore try to highlight some of the data of contemporary experience. Finally, I will offer some suggestions about the direction of our reflection and research at the service of a true renewal of our cycle of feasts and seasons.

Allow me one last introductory word. This has been a difficult presentation to put together, in part, I suppose, because the "liturgical year" for many Christians and even a good number of us who are professional liturgists is a fiction. The temptation in dealing with a "fiction" is to romanticize the past. The liturgical year may be a fiction now, but in the halcyon days of the early Church the liturgical year was alive and well. Why not recover those days? That is the temptation. But I trust that what follows is an exercise in candor rather than romanticism, a genuine attempt to reverence contemporary human experience as a source of theology. My motivation throughout has been captured in those marvelous lines from *A Thousand Clowns:* "You've got to know what day it is. You have to own your days and name them or else the years go right by and none of them belongs to you."

THE RELATIONSHIP OF THE LITURGICAL YEAR TO THE CIVIL CALENDAR

In 1949 H. Richard Niebuhr delivered a series of lectures at Austin Presbyterian Theological Seminary dealing with the relationship of Christ and culture or Christianity and civilization. Niebuhr called this the many-sided debate and the enduring problem for Christians. It sometimes dealt with broad questions of the Church's responsibility for the social order or of the need for a new separation of Christ's followers from the world. It was sometimes concentrated on particular issues as those of the place of Christian faith in general education or of Christian ethics in economic life. Niebuhr advanced this perennial debate by organizing the broad relationship of Christianity and culture in a typology of five "typical Christian answers" to the problem.

His lectures were subsequently printed and reprinted under the title *Christ and Culture.* [1] I believe his categories will be useful to us in exploring the special issue we face, namely, the relationship of the secular and ecclesiastical calendars. We will look in turn at the categories of opposition, identification, purification, paradox, and transformation.

Opposition. If we were to regard the relationship of our two calendars as that of opposition, then our position would be something like this: whatever the customs of society, whatever civil holidays, whatever cultural observances in time, we, as Christians, are opposed to them. It is a simple either-or position. This relationship of opposition seems operative in the earliest days of the Church both in the early Christians' antagonism to Jewish culture as well as Christians' flight from or assault upon Greco-Roman civilization. An example of this attitude forms part of the earliest ethos for the celebration of Sunday, the *dies solis*. The community saw in this symbolic name for Christ a way of neutralizing the increasingly popular religion of Mithras with its cult of the sun.

Identification. The opposite extreme of the relationship of opposition is that of identification. Identification involves the recognition of a fundamental convergence of Christ and culture or, in our terms, of sacred and secular festivity. Such identification is evident in the fourth-century fallout of Constantine's Edict of Toleration. Constantine's coronation was a liturgical legitimation of the political and economic establishment. In large measure our post-Constantinian Church has never lost its imperial triumphalism, nor has the imperial mark on its dress, behavior, use of space, lights and incense—in a word, in its style of festive celebration. The convergence of civil and ecclesiastical time under Constantine certainly facilitated the festive celebration of the Sunday liturgy, but another consequence was that the sabbath commandment of rest from work became increasingly a focal point. In addition, the cult of martyrs, the forerunners of our sanctoral cycle, was given a big boost by Constantine who built a magnificent basilica in honor of all the apostles, which was to serve as his own burial vault.

Opposition and identification are the two extremes. Opposition seems an appropriate response if the values of a given society are diametrically opposed to Christian values. This attitude, however, can miss the signs of salvation present within all of human life. On the other hand, the Christian and his or her celebration of time may become too wedded to the spirit of an age or its individual manifestations. On June 17, 1984, whether we pretend that Father's Day simply does not exist or whether we attempt to understand the mystery of the Trinity through the eyes of fathers, could be a consequence of taking one or another of these positions on the extreme.

Purification. There are three other positions which one might assume in relating the two experiences of time and calendar, each of them an attempt to mediate between these two extremes of opposition or total identification. The first of these mediating positions is purification, a way of viewing the relationship of sacred and secular much akin to that of identification. But while there is a certain amount of identification, there is also a way in which this particular mode of relationship views all of culture as but preparation for Christianity. All things Christian stand a little above culture. So, for example, the best of our civil year's sense of time and festivity as expressed in our feast of Thanksgiving is really but preparation for true Christian *eucharistia*. It will be the liturgical year that will come along and lift the civil year to a higher plane. Consider the Church's attempt to Christianize the celebration of labor on May Day. May 1 is lifted up and human labor is somehow "consecrated" by naming the day the feast of St. Joseph the Worker. Human labor and the dignity of human work become personified and purified in the person of St. Joseph.

Paradox. Yet another possible mode of relationship is that of paradox, a relationship akin to opposition but less stringent in its methods or its view of culture in general. The relationship of paradox says this: there is really *no* relationship between things cultural and things Christian. There are two totally separate spheres of reality, the sacral and the secular. In this view the civil and liturgical calendars are completely autonomous and liturgy thus becomes divorced from all contemporary cultural forms. This mode of relationship makes us citizens of two worlds with obedience due to God and to Caesar. We experience polarity and tension as we live in such a paradoxical relationship to Christ and to culture.

Now I would propose to you that a passage from Gelineau's *The Liturgy Today and Tomorrow* seems to come close to the paradox point of view:

If the church wants festivals, special times of the year, she must hold them with and within the community of believers without the support of society in general. Wasn't this also the case for the early church which lived in a pagan society, when the christian Sunday was not related to the civil calendar? The church today may be forced, in order to be able to celebrate its festivals as it wishes, to cut itself off from social customs which it created but which have now turned against it.[2]

Transformation. Finally, transformation is a fifth mode of relating the civil and ecclesial years. This view recognizes that Christ and Christianity are often antithetical to prevailing cultural trends and values, or, to speak in our terms, this position acknowledges that the inherent values expressed in civil and religious feasting may sometimes be diametrically opposed. But at the same time, the transformation position acknowledges that men and women are immersed in culture and society; that they live and move and have their being in civil times; that they are converted in time and are gradually transformed there or nowhere.

Niebuhr was quick to point out that the Gospel of St. John is a strong exponent of this transformation process: ". . . natural birth, eating, drinking, wind, water, and bread and wine are for this evangelist not only symbols to be employed in dealing with the realities of the life of the spirit but are (themselves) pregnant with spiritual meaning."[3]

When I ponder this position, and indeed as I choose it, I recall Teilhard de Chardin's words in the *Divine Milieu:* "By virtue of the Creation and, still more, of the Incarnation, *nothing* here below is *profane* for those who know how to see. On the contrary, everything is sacred to those capable of distinguishing that portion of chosen being which is subject to the attraction of Christ in the process of consummation."[4] But let there be no mistake.

To speak in these terms of a relationship of transformation is not in any way a simple kind of accommodation or of peaceful coexistence. Transformation is more radical than opposition or paradox; it is stronger and more rigorous in its implications than identification or purification.

In this view the Church cannot *not* proclaim its message in each culture and age, and, in the language and the accents of the age. The past heritage of the community continually is open to embracing new cultural expressions into its abundance. In this view the Church lives in a kind of creative tension in its relationship with culture, and the liturgical and civil calendars are in a relationship of dialogue because "spiritual and natural events are interlocking and analogous."[5]

This position of transformation, it seems to me, is exemplified in a suggestion made by Aidan Kavanagh several years ago in *Concilium:*

> If a Christian group is to correct its liturgical undernourishment by ingesting cultural elements patiently into its own *praxis* of covenant-faith in God through Christ, it must do so in the knowledge that, when it deals with symbolic patterns, not all these need be rendered overtly Christian in order to function for the group's good. Symbols abroad in a culture are unavoidable and thus always function to some degree. To be blunt about it, if there are functioning puberty rites or ceremonies of civil majority present in a given culture, there seems little reason why these have to be reproduced *within* the Christian community's sacramental-liturgical system. Rather, a more healthy policy might seek to take advantage of such external patterns simply by over-running them with faithful Christians who, in passing regularly through them, steadily purify them of connotations inimical to the Gospel and instill in them a sense of the creator's intent for all creation, human or otherwise.[6]

In summary, having explored a variety of ways to express the relationship between civil and ecclesiastical time and festivity, I propose that we adopt Niebuhr's category of transformation. Transformation is that mode of relationship which takes the incarnation seriously; which helps us to ponder God's work at the heart of human history and human experience; which leads us to discover that *nothing* is *profane*, for all human events and institutions are freighted with traces of the divine; and, finally, which urges us to seek always to discover and to release those human rhythms and cultural idioms which may serve as a vehicle for transformation into Christ.

CONTEMPORARY EXPERIENCE: LOCUS OF THEOLOGY

Let us turn now from these more theoretical considerations to an examination of contemporary human experience with regard to the liturgical year in order to note some of the potential or actual intersections of sacred and secular, to name possibilities for the transforming work of the Spirit, and, above all, to highlight those anomalous disparities between our official efforts at the renewal of liturgical time and the actual experience of people today. Let me preface our exploration of contemporary experience with a word about method.

The method I shall now outline is one which I call dialogical liturgical renewal, a fancy name for a simple procedure based on the European approach to pastoral theology. According to Rahner and others the primary concern of the pastoral theologian is the Church's coming-to-be in the concrete historical situation of today and tomorrow. Pastoral theology is motivated by a fundamental presupposition that the Church is a dynamic reality and that its communal life and growth are continually subject to and conditioned by the always-changing contemporary situation. Pastoral theology might even be called a theology of accommodation to the times. It offers a helpful procedure of reform which takes as its point of departure the contemporary context, which attempts to collect the data of human experience, to analyze them for meaning, to place them in dialogue with the living tradition of the community, and, finally, to formulate those forms of pastoral activity which will assist in the dynamic and continuous transformation of the community. Through this method, both tradition and culture are reverenced as two sources for theological reflection which need to be placed in dialogue. In the process the older is not necessarily regarded as the better (the romantic's view), nor, on the other hand, is the new and "relevant" necessarily regarded as responsible or faithful to the tradition.

I choose a pastoral-theological method to give shape to our discussion because it is most faithful to a "transformation" view of the relationship between the liturgical and civil years. Moreover, I am convinced that there is an odd note of unreality in this area of "liturgical year," which this pastoral method may alleviate. There is a gap between the concrete experience of contemporary American Roman Catholics and the explicit or implied expectation of the hiearchy and of pastoral liturgists alike, especially with regard to recovering a more authentic tradition—and the gap is becoming a chasm.

Now, let us attempt to gather the data, to name some facts and some experiences that we need to consider as we ponder the future of the liturgical year, its conflicts and challenges.

Fact: The liturgical year, experienced *as* a year, is fiction. If you ask a variety of people how they experience the liturgical year, they will tell you, as they have me during these last few weeks, that the liturgical year equals a disconnected series of feasts and seasons more or less meaningful to individuals. The liturgical year is not experienced in terms of linear time of a twelve-month duration.

Fact: Neither the liturgical year nor the civil year provides the rhythm by which almost all Americans live their lives. Our experience is dictated by an academic calendar; the real beginning of our year is the beginning of September; the feasts of our academic year are Labor Day and Memorial Day.

Fact: The liturgical calendar as a whole is the product of a Christian culture, and a culture that was rural, while the vast majority of Roman Catholics in the United States live in a post-Christian, urban environment, a fact which has profound implications for certain celebrations.

Fact: Sunday as the "original feast day," according to the Constitution on the Sacred Liturgy and as it is variously interpreted by commentators, is in real tension with: 1) the anticipation of Sunday on Saturday; 2) the larger experience of the weekend; 3) the variety of work and leisure patterns of Christians; 4) and the most basic experience, namely, that Sunday is not a day at all, but is constituted by a single hour of worship in many people's experience.

Fact: In the midst of the debate in the American Church concerning the number of Holy Days, with the understanding that some might be transferred to Sundays or eliminated from the calendar, Pope John Paul II proposes four more Holy Days of Obligation. This is a fact to be pondered along side the anthropological fact that feasts cannot be dictated but arise from the needs of the people.

Fact: The confusion and sometimes the casuistry which result when a Holy Day and a Sunday fall next to each other is beyond belief. The following caricature could rival Abbot and Costello's "Who's on first" routine:

You may fulfill your Mass obligation for the Holy Day by going on the preceding evening. You may go Friday evening for the Saturday Holy Day. For Sunday you may go Saturday evening, or you may go Saturday for the Holy Day and on Sunday for Sunday. You may also go Saturday for Saturday and Sunday for Sunday, except for Saturday evening which will be for Sunday. In other words you may go Friday and Saturday, or Friday and Sunday, or Saturday and Sunday, or twice on Saturday . . . . but you can't please all of the people all of the time. . . .

Fact: The calendar is still hopelessly crowded with saints' feasts and with obligatory and optional memorials. Our celebration of "that cloud of witnesses" remains, in general, a celebration of anonymous Christians which we observe if we happen to check the *ordo* and can find our way through the lectionary and the sacramentary.

Fact: We made a major mistake in moving certain feasts to new dates. We could have and should have learned from the moving of certain civil holidays to Mondays that amnesia sets in when a celebration is uprooted. For example, we only remember that it is Columbus Day when the mail is not delivered.

Fact: When Hallmark is successful in establishing a new feast and the entire country is caught up in caring enough to send the very best, the Church calendar cannot *not* acknowledge it. Whatever civil feast day is being observed, whether it is Mother's Day or Thanksgiving or Valentine's Day (we could probably draw the line at National Secretary's Day)—that is the point of departure for the transformation wrought by Christ. In this connection the most bizarre rubric in the sacramentary is that which precedes the votive Mass for the Beginning of the Civil Year: this Mass may not be celebrated on January 1.

Fact: The season of Lent touches something deep in our psyches and our souls, and Lent appears to be alive and well. However, Lent is entirely dependent for its meaning of a true catechumenate and a true order of penitents. Without a recovery of these ancient structures which bear profoundly contemporary meaning, Lent will be a quaint season containing disparate vestiges of other ages, bits and pieces from history, keepsakes like ashes and purple and penance and "giving up"—gradually becoming more and more unintelligible to the community.

Fact: While Lent may be alive and well, the great fifty days will probably never be "great." The Easter season appears to be prime vacation time for parish staffs rewarding themselves for surviving the triduum—not to mention the spring migration of parish musicians to the gathering of the National Association of Pastoral Musicians. In tandem with this fact, perhaps a question should be posed: are fifty days too long to sustain the Easter experience?

Fact: Advent remains for us in the Northern Hemisphere synchronous with nature, the shorter days, the great winter solstice. In other words, Advent as a season is supported and sustained by cosmic time in a way in which our other feasts and seasons have become immune. (I do not except the spring equinox from this statement, since air conditioning, the growing of plants indoors all year long, and the fluctuating date of Easter tend to immunize the community from the natural symbolism which supports and sustains the celebration of the paschal mystery.) Such powerful cosmic symbolism as the winter solstice provides may yet rescue Advent from the commercial exploitation of the number of shopping days before Christmas, and thus rescue Christmas as well, to the extent that it needs rescuing.

Fact: Ordinary Time is critical to human experience. There is no celebration without the backdrop of ordinariness. But ordinary need not mean "same," as, in general, it does mean now from Trinity Sunday to Advent.

Fact: When a group of people become concerned about particular issues, they talk about them and sometimes take action such as public demonstrations, marches, sit-ins, and so on. The recent "March on Washington" was such an event. This fact may suggest two things to us: first, that there *may* be a place for carefully planned national awareness campaigns within the Sunday assembly; and second, it may be a ripe moment to reinstate contemporary versions of the ancient disciplines of ember and rogation days, that is, some days of public prayer and penance for pressing issues of peace and justice.

FURTHER RESEARCH AND REFLECTION

Such are only a few of the facts which we can glean from contemporary experience. A more extended and rigorous survey would have to include data concerning familial celebrations, birthdays, anniversaries, certain ethnic observances, particular paired celebrations such as Halloween and All Saints or Mardi Gras and Ash Wednesday, the manner in which the meanings of some feasts and seasons modulate over time, the relative success of Congress in establishing national weeks for this and that, and so on. The questions at this early stage of research would remain: what can we learn from contemporary experience about time and festivity.

Ideally, we would next submit each of these facts to a more precise analysis with the particular assistance of the human sciences. Then we would attempt to interpret our refined "facts" in light of the tradition, the historical and theological development of the liturgical year. Finally, we would be in a position of advocacy and would be able to formulate forms of pastoral activity to assist the life and growth of the community. Several key areas call for our further research and reflection.

First, the area of the year. Initially, I would like to suggest that we abandon the terminology of "the liturgical year" in favor of a more accurate designation such as "liturgical feasts and seasons" or "the liturgical cycle of celebrations," designations which might more faithfully reflect the community's experience of ecclesial time and festivity, even as we begin to probe the real community experience of "year."

Earlier I implied that the community observes neither the civil calendar nor the ecclesial calendar but operates according to the rhythms of the academic year. This remark is not confined to time as experienced by students or parents or teachers: clothing manufacturers know it; T.V. networks observe it; parishes gear up or wind down because of it. If it is true that the academic year represents the natural rhythm of the community, perhaps in some measure our cycle of feasts and seasons needs to acknowledge this rhythm and to accommodate this experience of time, of new beginnings, of completion and joyous endings, and of certain shadow experiences inherent in both. Our ancestors lived by the rhythms of nature and experienced the cosmic powers and potential dangers of the seasons. I believe it is not too fanciful to see an analogue in the natural rhythm and potential dangers of the academic year. Think, for example, of Memorial Day as marking the beginning of summer and with it children no longer secure in a classroom, young adults out on the streets, greater unemployment and higher crime—critical experiences in urban culture analogous to natural crises in rural life.

Labor Day and Memorial Day are fixed dates in the civil calendar which enclose this "season." How should they be observed by Christians? Is there a way to bless these beginnings and endings? Is there a way to celebrate the true liminal quality of the summer months with their potential for transformation? Is there a way to prepare for these several feasts?

(In this connection it may be worthwhile to consider parenthetically how the celebration of our academic beginnings and endings might introduce diversity into the five-month expanse of Ordinary Time after Trinity Sunday. A series of three or four Sundays might be set aside to prepare for the beginning of the academic year, days when the community might call to mind those concerns which will motivate it during the year. I am speaking now of coming to terms with the perennial problem of "national awareness Sundays" in a way that is both realistic and creative. This implies long-range planning at the national and diocesan level, using the lectionary's readings and the sacramentary's prayers as point of departure in the planning process.)

I believe we have not even begun to understand what role the academic year plays in our experience of time, nor what potential it holds as a vehicle for the manifestation of the paschal mystery or the deepening of the Christian life.

While "year" is underexamined in this regard, Sunday may be just the opposite. There has been a great deal of research on the history and theology of Sunday and on probing the spirituality of Sunday. Often we look to the early Church for inspiration and direction in our effort to recover Sunday as the "original feast day." Occasionally Sunday becomes the focus of a diatribe about the secularizing tendencies of our age. All of this is true because Christians "live by the Lord's Day." Sunday is a symbol of a way of living.

As Mark Searle has surely developed this to your complete satisfaction, I want only to add one note. Sunday will continue to frustrate us as "the original feast day" unless and until we look at the contemporary human experience of the weekend and recognize one of its most positive implications for the experience of and enhancement of Sunday. What some anthropologists and social critics develop in detail is the change of activity which occurs over the weekend, the radically different experience of an approach to *time*. There is the pervasive sense that what I do on the weekend is optional and free. I am released from my weekday need to work for a salary, on a schedule determined by others, in what I may regard as an enslaving task or in a manner pragmatic and efficient. On the weekend I am free to do what I am doing; I experience liberation with regard to the use of time.

I believe that liberation or "liberated time" could be for us a prime symbol for understanding the paschal mystery, the mystery of redemption and liberation and new life. I am suggesting that we take peoples' actual experience of their use of time and its renewing and recreating aspects and make that the point of departure for a new understanding of God's liberating work in Jesus. I do not mean to suggest that this in any way exhausts the meaning of Sunday for us. I am proposing that probing the human experience of time for its deeper implications and meaning is one more way of reverencing the transforming presence and power of God in human life.

Finally, a very brief word about feasts as another fertile topic for continued reflection and research. Feasts have always been one of the community's ways of telling its story, whether we are referring to birthdays or anniversaries or the Thanksgiving or Christmas family gathering or feasting the saints. Feasts are our way of stepping outside ordinary time, of engaging with those we love and live with in a rite of passage or a significant moment in the life of one of our members. Feasts are celebrations of excess, moments in the process of living together which we share with a certain intensity, which bond us together, which make our world more human. On feasts we acknowledge that there are people and events which have shaped our life and inspired our future and which help us to live more consciously in the present because we have been able to proclaim "this is where we have been, who we are now, and where we are going."

Serious empirical research into the patterns of family feasting might have profound implications for ecclesial feasting in the following areas: the number of feasts a community can actually celebrate; the appropriate spacing of feasts; the possibility of devising true local calendars; the questions of obligation; the possibility of a single celebration of some dates rather than the fragmenting of the community; and above all the necessity of knowing the story which is being proclaimed in all manner of symbolic activity.

There is so much more I would love to explore. Indeed, when we accept that the relationship between the civil and ecclesial calendars is that of transformation, the exploring will be endless, the wealth of contemporary human experience will be overpowering, and the possibilities of faithful celebration of the saving work of God in Jesus will be profoundly enriched. Robert Taft captured this dialogue between tradition and contemporary experience better than I:

> There is no ideal model of Christian feast or calendar which we must "discover" and to which we must "return." Rather,

it is up to each generation to do what the Apostolic Church did in the very composition of the New Testament: apply the mystery and meaning of Christ to the *Sitz im Leben* of today. A liturgy is successful not because of its fidelity to some past ideal, but because it builds up the Body of Christ into a spiritual temple and priesthood by forwarding the aim of Christian life: the love and service of God and neighbor; death to self in order to live for others as did Christ.[7]

NOTES

1. N. Richard Niebuhr, *Christ and Culture* (New York: Harper Torchbooks, 1951). Niebuhr does not use the relationship of the liturgical and civil years as an example of his work; the interpretation and application of his categories to this topic are mine.

2. Joseph Gelineau, *The Liturgy Today and Tomorrow*, trans. Dinah Livingstone (New York: Paulist Press, 1978) 62.

3. Niebuhr, *Christ and Culture* 197.

4. Pierre Teilhard de Chardin, *The Divine Milieu* (New York: Harper and Brothers, 1960) 35.

5. Niebuhr, *Christ and Culture* 197.

6. Aidan Kavanagh, "Life Cycle Events, Civil Ritual and the Christian," in Power and Maldonado, *Liturgy and Human Passage*, Concilium CXII (New York: Seabury, 1979) 22.

7. Robert Taft, "The Liturgical Year: Studies, Prospects, Reflections," *Worship* LV (1981) 22.

CONTRIBUTORS

MARK SEARLE is the associate director of the Notre Dame Center for Pastoral Liturgy and an associate professor at the University of Notre Dame. He has an S.T.L. from the Pontifical Athenaeum of S. Antonio in Rome, a diploma in Liturgical Studies from the Liturgical Institute at Trier, and a doctorate in theology from the Theological Faculty, Trier. Dr. Searle is a consultant to ICEL and is a past president of the North American Academy of Liturgy (1983–1984). He has written and lectured extensively in liturgy and sacramental theology.

TAD GUZIE is a professor of religious education at the University of Calgary in Canada. He received a Ph.D. from the University of Cambridge. A frequent lecturer throughout North America, he has conducted workshops for teachers, liturgical leaders, and pastoral ministers. His latest book is *Sacramental Basics* (Paulist Press).

PATRICK REGAN, O.S.B., is the abbot of St. Joseph Abbey in St. Benedict, Louisiana. He holds an M.A. in sacred liturgy and a doctorate of sacred theology from the Institut Catholique in Paris. Abbot Regan has written numerous articles, conducted workshops, and has taught liturgy at the graduate school of St. John's University in Collegeville. Since 1973 he has been an associate editor of *Worship*.

KATHLEEN HUGHES, R.C.S.J., is an assistant professor of liturgy at the Catholic Theological Union in Chicago. She has an M.A. and a Ph.D. in liturgical studies from the University of Notre Dame. She serves on the advisory board of ICEL, where she chairs the Subcommittee on Original Texts. Her articles have appeared in *Celebration, Modern Liturgy, New Catholic World*, and *Pastoral Music*.